John R. Sweney

The Garner

Songs and Hymns for Sundayschools, Prayer Meetings, Temperance, and Gospel

Meetings

John R. Sweney

The Garner

Songs and Hymns for Sundayschools, Prayer Meetings, Temperance, and Gospel Meetings

ISBN/EAN: 9783743417748

Manufactured in Europe, USA, Canada, Australia, Japa

Cover: Foto ©Thomas Meinert / pixelio.de

Manufactured and distributed by brebook publishing software (www.brebook.com)

John R. Sweney

The Garner

THE ARNER

Songs and Hymns

FOR

SUNDAY-SCHOOLS,
PRAYER MEETINGS,
TEMPERANCE, AND
GOSPEL MEETINGS.

TOGETHER WITH

Elementary Instruction and Exercises,

FOR MUSIC CLASSES.

BY

JOHN R. SWENEY, M.B.

Philadelphia :
PUBLISHED BY JOHN J. HOOD, 608 ARCH ST.

PREFACE.

THE GARNER is so named because it is believed to contain only carefully winnowed song-wheat. We have herein endeavored to give poetical expression to the varied phases of Christian experience, and to meet the musical requirements of the most important departments of Christian work and usefulness.

The Elementary Department forms a feature which we believe will be welcomed by many who have at heart the advancement of musical knowledge in Church or Sunday School. The method of instruction here adopted is one that has been fully tested, and has proved to be the easiest and best for teaching vocal music. With a view to greater simplicity, and the improvement of the system, a few departures have been made from the usual technicalities of musical instruction; we trust their value will be seen and appreciated by the intelligent musician.

We take this opportunity of thanking those friends who have kindly aided us in our work by original contributions, or who have granted the use of valuable copyrights.

JOHN R. SWENEY,
Editor.
JOHN J. HOOD,
Publisher.

ELEMENTARY DEPARTMENT.

CONSISTING OF

Rules, Examples, and Exercises, for the Use of Singing-Classes.

By J. J. H.

GENERAL RULES FOR CORRECT SINGING.

THE singer should be in an *upright* position, the shoulders to be held back, and rather down, the head somewhat elevated. The mouth should be *freely open*, but without extreme gaping. Expand the chest until the ribs at the side press against the clothes; by compressing the muscles of the abdomen, and at first breathing frequently, but in the right places, the pupil will soon learn to keep the chest always expanded while singing. Deliver the tones freely, without interruption from the throat, tongue, teeth, or lips; let the lower notes be firm and full, the higher clear and soft, always taking care not to strain the voice beyond its natural limits. Correct pronunciation is important; when the words are clearly uttered the music has much greater charms for the listener; let the consonants be sharply expressed, not dwelt upon; the vowel sound of a syllable being the most musical part, is best suited for singing; strike the true vowel sound as quickly, and retain it as long as possible, letting the consonants come as it were *between* the notes. The consonants are the *strong* parts of a syllable, they should be *emphasized* as the proper expression of the sentiment may require.

The most effective singing, and that which affords most pleasure and profit to both the singer and the listener, is that which truly expresses the emotions of the heart. Always try to *feel* the sentiment you would express; the power of music belongs to the heart, it can only reach the heart when it flows from the heart. Above all, let a sacred theme be sung in a becoming spirit; nor let the worship of God be as

" Idle words
Upon an idle tongue."

THE ALPHABET OF MUSIC.

In learning to read music, as in learning to read words, the pupil must first become familiar with the alphabet. The musical alphabet, or Scale, consists of seven sounds, each having a distinctive character. The pupil should as early as possible become familiar with the mental effect, or *character*, of each of these seven sounds; he will thereby be able to recognize any note when heard, or sing the true sound on seeing the sign in written music by which it is represented.

The diagram of the Vocal Scale on next page gives the names of these sounds as they are usually *pronounced;* they are all from the Italian, with the exception of *Ze*, which has been altered from *Se* in order to have a different initial letter for each syllable. The relative position, or *pitch*, of the sounds is shown, with as near a description of their characters as can be given in words. Like the colors of the rainbow, to which these seven sounds in some respects bear a close resemblance, their effects on the mind are *felt*, yet cannot be fully described. To bring out these qualities, it is necessary to hear the sounds in their relation to each other. If one note be heard alone, the memory of no other note being in the ear, it has no such mental effect; but let other notes be heard, bearing a *key relationship* to each other, and *Doh* will then become what is known as the *Key note*, and its character one of rest, *Ray* will become the stirring, or rousing note, *Ze* the restless or piercing note, etc. Prove this by listening to these effects as heard in tunes; notice also that only the note of rest, which is the key-note, *Doh*, can fully satisfy the ear at the close of a tune.

The Teacher will readily find illustrations of " mental effect " in the following Exercises; point out these characteristics also while using the Exercises. The syllable *Ze* should be pronounced *tze*.

EXERCISES ON THE VOCAL SCALE.

In the following Exercises the first letters only of the Sol fa syllables are used. At this stage use only the Sol fa portion of the Exercises. Repeat until familiar with the sound of each note, then use the open syllable *lah*. Point with a pencil to the note, while singing, on the Vocal Scale. It is of great importance that the pupil should become thoroughly acquainted with each note, and its position on the Vocal Scale. When the Scale has become pictured in the mind, and the character and position of each note has become familiar to the ear, the greatest difficulty in the path of the young singer will have been overcome, and singing by note will be accomplished by easy and pleasant practice. Teachers of classes should be furnished with a large Vocal Scale,* and spend a portion of each lesson in pointing exercises and tunes, the class singing as he points.

THE VOCAL SCALE.

After practising Exercises 4 and 5, divide the class into two sections; while one section sings No. 4, let the other sing No. 5. Again, let one section repeat each note thus, d d, while the other sings one d.

*For a Vocal Scale Chart, suitable for classes, address the publisher of this work.

EXERCISES ON THE VOCAL SCALE.

The note *lah* is introduced in Ex. 7; its mournful character will readily be noticed.

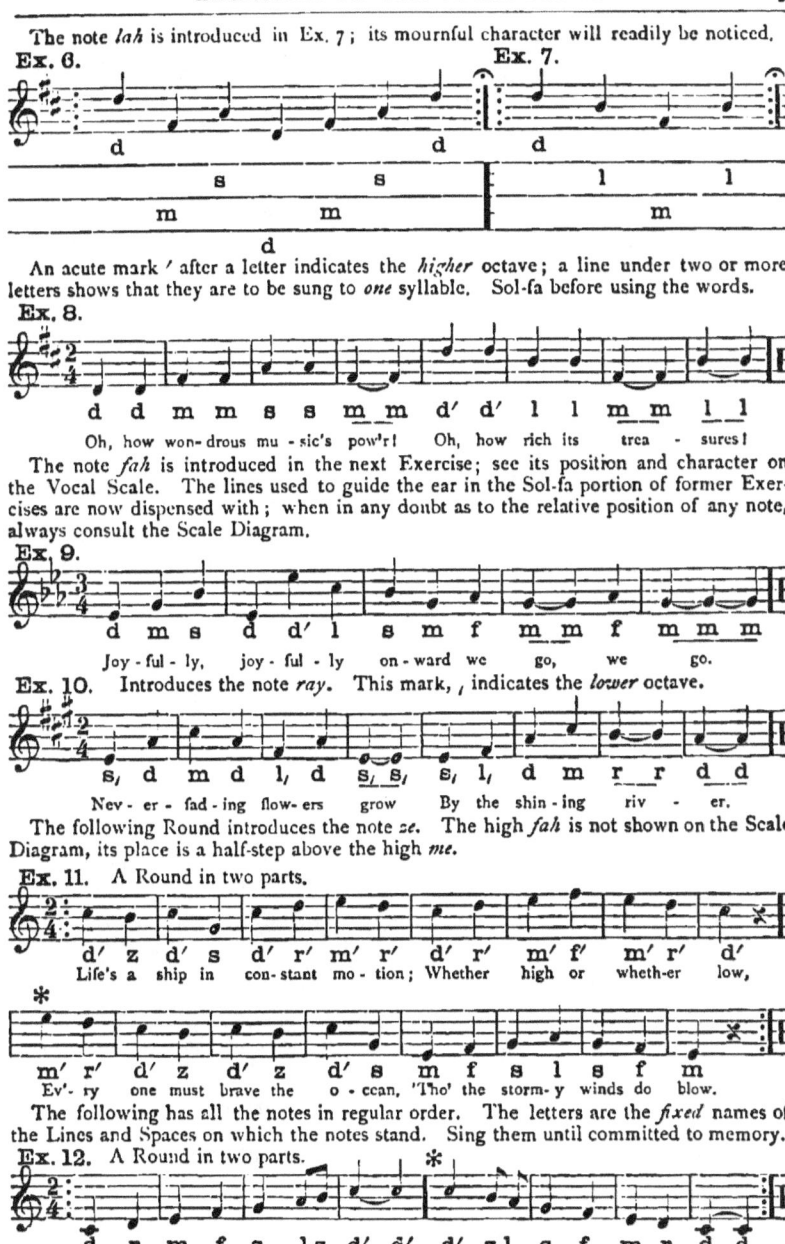

An acute mark ′ after a letter indicates the *higher* octave; a line under two or more letters shows that they are to be sung to *one* syllable. Sol-fa before using the words.

The note *fah* is introduced in the next Exercise; see its position and character on the Vocal Scale. The lines used to guide the ear in the Sol-fa portion of former Exercises are now dispensed with; when in any doubt as to the relative position of any note, always consult the Scale Diagram.

Ex. 10. Introduces the note *ray*. This mark, , indicates the *lower* octave.

The following Round introduces the note *ze*. The high *fah* is not shown on the Scale Diagram, its place is a half-step above the high *me*.

Ex. 11. A Round in two parts.

The following has all the notes in regular order. The letters are the *fixed* names of the Lines and Spaces on which the notes stand. Sing them until committed to memory.

Ex. 12. A Round in two parts.

THE STAFF, CLEFS, &c.

The main purpose of the Exercises hitherto has been to teach the Notes of the Scale. Let the Teacher supplement each Exercise by practice on the Vocal Scale Chart, giving the new note in a variety of positions. The Exercises may be divided into Lessons as follows,—First Lesson, Ex. 1, 2, 3, 4, 5, 6; Second Lesson, Ex. 7, 8, 9; Third Lesson, Ex. 10, 11, 12. Having mastered the Scale, the pupil will now be ready to know how it is represented on the Music Staff.

STAFF WITH LEDGER LINES.

```
                    2d ledger line ── above the staff.
                    1st        do   ──           do.
─────────────────────────────────────────────────────────── 5th line ───
──────────────────────────────────── 4th line ──── 4th space ──────────
───────────────────── 2d line ─── 3d space ────────────────────────────
──────── 1st space ── 2d space ──── 2d line ──────────────────────────
── 1st line ──────────────────────────────────────────────────────────
                    1st ledger line ── below the staff.
                    2d         do.   ──           do.
```

The STAFF consists of five parallel Lines, and the four Spaces between.

Small lines, called LEDGER LINES, are added above or below the Staff, as the music may require.

In counting the Lines or Spaces of the Staff, begin at the lowest, and count *upwards*; count the Ledger Lines *from* the Staff, upwards or downwards.

Every line and space is a Degree of the Staff. From one line or space to the next line or space is the Second Degree, always counting the one started from as the First. The same applies to the Notes of the Scale; *ray* is the Second Degree above *doh, me* the Third, &c.

CLEFS, AND *FIXED* NAMES OF THE LINES AND SPACES.

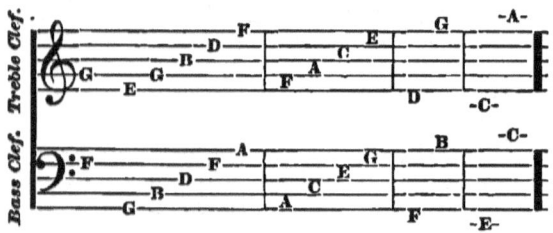

The first seven letters of the alphabet are used in naming the lines and spaces of the Staff; there are two principal ways of applying the letters, denoted by the CLEF placed at the beginning of the Staff.

The TREBLE CLEF (also named the G CLEF) places the letters on the Staff so that G falls on the second line. In vocal music this Clef is used chiefly in female voice parts.

The BASS CLEF (named also the F CLEF) places the letters on the Staff so that F falls on the fourth line. In vocal music this Clef is used in male voice parts.

The C CLEF, makes the line or space, lying within the heavy lines, C; the pitch being the same as that of the C of the first ledger line below the Treble Staff. The C Clef is used in modern music books chiefly to distinguish the Tenor Part, and is commonly, in such cases, placed on the third space, thus making the names of the lines and spaces the same as on the Treble Staff, but the real pitch eight degrees lower.

RELATIVE POSITION OF THE BASS AND TREBLE STAVES.

The first ledger line above the Bass Staff is C, and is identical in pitch with the C of the first ledger line below the Treble Staff; the two staves are thus connected by one ledger line, as in the following example. The name of Middle C is sometimes given to this ledger line, being used as a standard for denominating the pitch of other letters, as, "— above Middle C," or "— below Middle C."

POSITIONS OF THE VOCAL SCALE ON THE STAFF.

THE USES OF SHARPS, FLATS, Etc.

The Vocal Scale contains twelve half-steps. A half-step is the distance in pitch between the notes *me* and *fah*, also between *ze* and *doh'*; between any other adjoining notes the natural distance is one step, or two half steps.

The letters under the above diagram represent the staff-names. The natural intervals between the degrees of the Staff also consist of steps and half-steps, as shown above. If the notes of the Scale be placed on the Staff so that the note *doh* will come on C, then all the intervals of the Scale will correspond with those of the Staff. Music so written is said to be in the *Natural Key.*

But this position or pitch of the Scale will not meet the wants of every class of tunes; in nine cases out of ten it is necessary to have the Key-note, or *doh*, either higher or lower than C. This necessitates, in such cases, a re-adjustment of the staff-intervals; the following shows the alterations necessary when the Key-note is placed on D:—

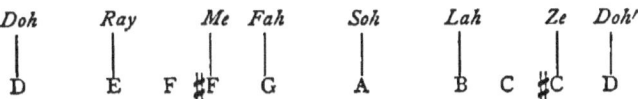

It will be seen that the staff-interval between E and F does not correspond with the scale-interval between *ray* and *me*, the same dissimilarity exists between B and C and the notes *lah* and *ze*; to remedy this irregularity, a SHARP (♯) is employed, the use of which is to raise the letter on which it is placed by one half-step,—bringing the note a half-step nearer the note immediately above, and the same distance farther from the note below. This is shown in the following example:—

Placed on the Staff, the above example will appear as under. Sharps are placed on the line and space represented by F and C, at the beginning of the Staff, thereby effecting all the notes on that line or space throughout the Staff.

Another method of regulating the intervals of Staff and Scale is by *lowering* the staff-letters a half-step, instead of raising them, as in former examples; this is done by the use of a FLAT (♭). By placing the key-note, *doh*, on F, we will illustrate this method:—

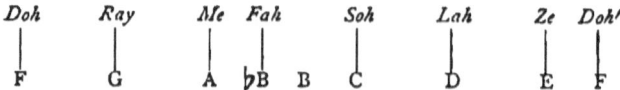

On the Staff, the above example will appear as under. A Flat is placed on the line represented by the letter B.

As many as five Flats, or the same number of Sharps, are sometimes necessary to make all the intervals of the Staff and Scale correspond. These are placed immediately after the Clef at the beginning of the Staff, and form the KEY SIGNATURE.

ACCIDENTALS.

Any alteration of the pitch of a letter throughout the Staff, not provided for by the Key-signature, is termed an ACCIDENTAL.

A SHARP ♯ placed before any note throughout the Staff raises its pitch by one half-step.

A FLAT ♭ placed before any note throughout the Staff lowers its pitch by one half-step.

A NATURAL ♮ *cancels* any Sharp or Flat that may have been employed on the line or space on which it is placed, restoring the same to its natural pitch.

When a letter has already been sharped, and it is required to raise it still another half-step, a DOUBLE SHARP ✕ is employed. If after being flatted it is required to lower a note still another half-step, a DOUBLE FLAT ♭♭ is used.

An Accidental effects all notes of the same name within the measure in which it occurs; but when an altered note is *continued* in the next measure, it still retains the accidental form.

RULES FOR FINDING THE KEY-NOTE.

The TREBLE CLEF places the Key-note, *doh*, on the Third Space.

The BASS CLEF places the Key-note, *doh*, on the Second Space.

The TENOR CLEF places the Key-note, *doh*, on the Third Space.

One SHARP after a Clef indicates that the Line or Space on which it is placed is *ze;* the Line or Space immediately above being the Key-note.

If more than one SHARP be placed after the Clef, the one *farthest* from the Clef indicates that the Line or Space on which it is placed is *ze;* the Line or Space immediately above is the Key-note.

One FLAT after a Clef indicates that the Line or Space on which it is placed is *fah;* the fifth degree above, or the fourth degree below, is the Key-note.

If more than one FLAT be placed after a Clef, the one *farthest* from the Clef indicates that the Line or Space on which it is placed is *fah;* the fifth degree above, or the fourth degree below, is the Key-note.

The Teacher should require the pupils to find illustrations of each of the above paragraphs, by reference to compositions throughout the following pages.

ACCENT, MEASURE, AND TIME.

Time Signatures.   Bar.   Measure.   Bar.   Double Bar.   Closing Bar.

The length, or duration, of notes is measured by *pulses*, or *beats*. Pulses are arranged in equal groups according to the laws of rhythm. The number of pulses in each group is governed by the recurrence of the accent. The groups are separated by Bars; from one bar to the next is called a Measure; the pulse following the bar is the *accented* pulse.

| Bright-est and | best of the | sons of the | morn-ing, |

In the above line of poetry the accent is on every third syllable; this illustrates what in music is known as Triple Measure, each measure consisting of *three* pulses.

All | peo-ple | that on | earth do | dwell, |

Here the accent is on every *second* syllable, and in music corresponds to what is known as Double Measure, each measure consisting of *two* pulses.

From Double Measure and Triple Measure are derived a variety of others, based upon them: from the first named is derived Quadruple Measure, having *four* pulses; from the last named we have Compound Triple Measure, having *nine* pulses: from a combination of both are derived Compound Double Measure, having *six* pulses; and Compound Quadruple Measure, having *twelve* pulses.

The class of Measure in which a composition is written is denoted at the beginning by two figures, arranged in the form of a fraction; in the Time Signatures at the top of this page all the varieties are represented; by the upper figure is shown the number of *pulses* contained in the Measure, the under figure indicates the kind of note that represents *one* pulse or beat. The under figure may be either 2, 4, or 8, according to the kind of note used to represent one pulse, but this does not alter the *character* of the Measure.

MEASURES.

The strong accent follows the bar in all classes of measures; in Quadruple Measure, a secondary accent is given to the *third* pulse; in all Compound measures a slight accent is given to the first pulse in each group of three, as they are shown above.

* Quadruple Measure also receives the name of Common Time, and is sometimes designated by a letter C in the signature; if the C has a perpendicular line through its centre, two pulses only are given to the measure.

METHODS OF COUNTING AND BEATING TIME.

Pulses are measured by counting, or by motions of the right hand. In counting, always begin with the first pulse of the measure, repeating the same numbers for each succeeding measure, as, for Double Measure, 1 2, 1 2, 1 2; for Triple Measure, 1 2 3, 1 2 3, 1 2 3; In measuring time by beats of the right hand, the movements are, for Double Measure, 1st down, 2d up; for Triple Measure, 1st down, 2d left, 3d up; for Quadruple Measure, 1st down, 2d left, 3d right, 4th up. The down beat follows the bar, and is always on the accented pulse. These motions also serve for Compound Measures, by giving three parts to each beat.

NOTES AND RESTS.

NOTES have two uses:—by their *position* on the staff, to show the pitch of tones; by their *shape*, to indicate the length or duration of tones. The Notes in common use are,

The relative time values of these Notes are as two to one, in the order given above:— one Whole Note is equal to two Half Notes, one Half Note is equal to two Quarter Notes, etc. Also, one Whole is equal to four Quarters, or eight Eighths, or sixteen Sixteenths.

A DOT placed after any Note lengthens it by one-half: thus, a Dotted Whole is equal to three Halfs, a Dotted Half is equal to three Quarters, etc. Two Dots lengthen the Note after which they are placed by one-half and one-fourth, (or by three-fourths).

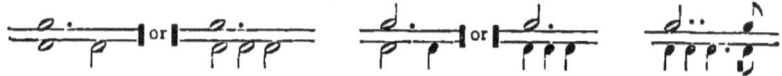

RESTS are characters used to indicate *silence;* by their various shapes and positions are shown how long silence is to continue. Each Note has a corresponding Rest.

The relative time values of Rests are the same as above applied to Notes: this may be further illustrated thus, if a Whole lasts during four pulses or beats, then a Half lasts during two, a Quarter during one, an Eighth during one-half pulse, a Sixteenth during one-quarter pulse. This illustration is borrowed from a Quadruple Measure; in other kinds of measure the Whole may receive a greater or less number of pulses, but the proportions are the same in each.

EXERCISES IN TIME AND MEASURE.

The number of pulses is shown by the number of Sol-fa letters under each note.

Ex. 13. Double Measure. One sharp; *doh* is on G.

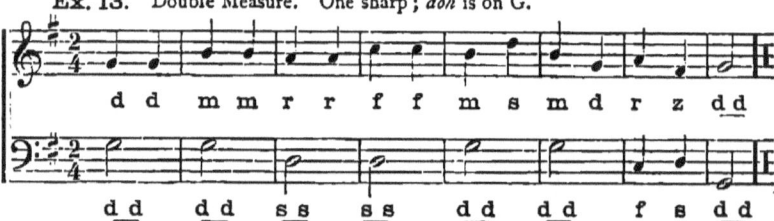

Ex. 14. Quadruple Measure. One flat, *doh* is on F.

EXERCISES IN TIME AND MEASURE.

Ex. 15. Triple Measure. *Doh* is on G.

Ex. 16. Compound Double Measure. Three sharps, *doh* is on A.

When the first notes of a strain of music do not make a complete measure, the time is taken from the last measure of the strain.

Ex. 17. Compound Triple Measure. Two flats, *doh* is on B flat.

The Whole Rest is also used to indicate a rest of one measure of any kind. Two Sol-fa letters joined by a hyphen indicate that the two notes are to receive but one pulse.

Ex. 18. Measure Rests. Half-pulse notes. Dotted note. Tied notes.

Ex. 19. Two sharps, *doh* is on D. Quarter Rests.

```
d- m    r- f  m- s   f- l   s      d  z- l   s s- f   m   r   d d
d- m    r- f       m- s   f- l   s      m  s- f   m m- r   d   z   d d
```

THE CHROMATIC SCALE.

In Ex. 17 a note is used that does not belong to the Vocal Scale, the note *fe*, this is an intermediate note between *fah* and *soh*. In this instance it is used as a Chromatic passing note. Between the notes of the Vocal Scale that are separated by a full step, (*doh ray, ray me, fah soh, soh lah,* and *lah ze,*) a Chromatic note may be used. A Scale having all its notes separated by a half-step may be formed, which will include every possible intermediate note. This is named the CHROMATIC SCALE. Each intermediate note may be formed in two ways: 1st, the principal note beneath may be sharped; 2d, the principal note above may be flatted. By the system of naming the notes of the scale adopted in this work, we are enabled not only to use a separate initial letter for each note, but to give a distinct name to every possible variation thereof. The following diagrams give the Chromatic Scale formed in the two ways above-mentioned. Notice the rule,—when a note is sharped, the final vowel is changed to *e;* when flatted, the final vowel is changed to *a* or *au*. Thus, *soh* when sharped becomes *se*, when flatted, it becomes *sau*.

ASCENDING, BY SHARPS.

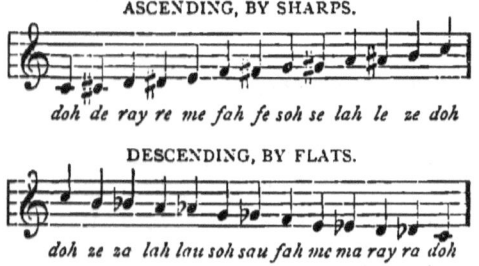

doh de ray re me fah fe soh se lah le ze doh

DESCENDING, BY FLATS.

doh ze za lah lau soh sau fah me ma ray ra doh

SHARPS		FLATS
DOH		DOH
ZE		ZE
le		za
LAH		LAH
se		lau
SOH		SOH
fe		sau
FAH		FAH
ME		ME
re		ma
RAY		RAY
de		ra
DOH		DOH

The note *fe* is the most frequently used of the intermediate notes; besides being a chromatic passing note, forming a bridge between the notes *fah* and *soh*, it is also used in modulating, or changing the key-note, from *doh* to *soh*,--that is, the note which formerly was *soh*, for a time becomes *doh*, the note *fe* taking the position of a new *ze*, or leading note, to the new key-note. This modulation, or change of key-note takes place in a large proportion of tunes. By the use of the intermediate notes, representing sharps or flats as the case may require, the key-note may be changed to any desired note; when, however, such changes are made, the laws of Composition require that the original key-note be returned to at or before the close of the composition.

After *fe*, the next intermediate note in frequency of occurrence is *se*, the sharp form of *soh;* it always occurs when the MINOR KEY, or key of *Lah*, is introduced, where *se* becomes the leading note to *lah*, the minor key-note. This may be observed in the following Minor Scale.

THE MINOR SCALE.

SOME difficulty is experienced, under various systems of teaching music, in giving a correct idea of what is termed the Minor Scale; but if the pupil will look on it and study it simply as that portion of the Vocal Scale (or Major Scale) from *lah* to *lah'*, much of the difficulty will be avoided. It is important to remember that in minor compositions *lah* is the key-note, and that when the key of a piece is minor, as, for example, D minor, *lah* is on D; *doh* will then be on F, and the same Signature will be used as for a composition in F major. The two keys are said to be *relative* to each other. Hence, the Signature of any Minor Key is the same as that of its Relative Major. Notice in the following scale that, in ascending, the sixth and seventh notes are sharped.

MINOR SCALE, ASCENDING AND DESCENDING.

lah ze doh ray me fe se lah   lah soh fah me ray doh ze lah

VOICES.

THE Compasses of the two main divisions of the human voice are given on page 7; they are further sub-divided as follows: high female voices, SOPRANO; low female voices, ALTO; high male voices, TENOR; low male voices, BASS. Young boys' voices belong to the female division.

MISCELLANEOUS.

Repeat. Sign. Pause. Slur. Tie. Bind. Triplet. Staccato. Sforzando.

Diminuend. Crescendo.   Swell.   First ending. Second ending.

A LIST OF MUSICAL TERMS.

ALLEGRO. Fast.
BIND. Two notes on the same degree to be sung as one.
CHORUS. *Cho.* A full-voiced refrain after each stanza.
CODA. A final ending.
CON ESPRESS. With expression.
CRESCENDO. *cres.* Gradually increase in power.
DA CAPO. *D.C.* From the beginning.
DAL SEGNO. *D.S.* From the sign.
DIMINUENDO. *dim.* Diminish in force, to become gradually softer.
FINE. The finish.
FORTE. *f.* Loud.
FORTISSIMO. *ff* Very loud.
MEZZO, (metz'o), *m.* With medium voice, neither loud nor soft.
MEZZO FORTE. *mf.* Medium loud.
MEZZO PIANO. *mp.* Medium soft.
MAESTOSO. Majestically.
MODERATO. Moderate speed.
PAUSE. Dwell on the note.

PIANISSIMO. *pp.* Very soft.
PIANO. *p.* Soft.
RALLENTANDO. *rall.* Slacken time, and decrease in force.
REFRAIN. A repetition of the last line or idea of each stanza.
REPEAT. Sing the same portion twice.
RITARDANDO. *rit.* Slacken the time.
SFORZANDO. *sf.* With extra force.
SIGN. A mark used to show where a repeat begins.
SLUR. Sing the notes to one syllable.
STACCATO. Short and detached.
SWELL. First increasing, then diminishing, in power.
TEMPO. In the original time.
TIE. A form of joining Eighth, Sixteenth, or Thirty-second notes.
TRIPLET. Three notes to be sung in the time of two.
ZE (pronounced *tze*). The name given to the seventh note of the scale; adopted for the first time in the present work.

14. Come Quick and Take Me O'er.

Lines suggested by some of the last words of Mrs. Anna S. Allen.
Surely I come quickly; Amen. Even so, come, Lord Jesus.—Rev. xxii. 20.

Mrs. CLEMENTINE E. HOWES.   WM. J. KIRKPATRICK.

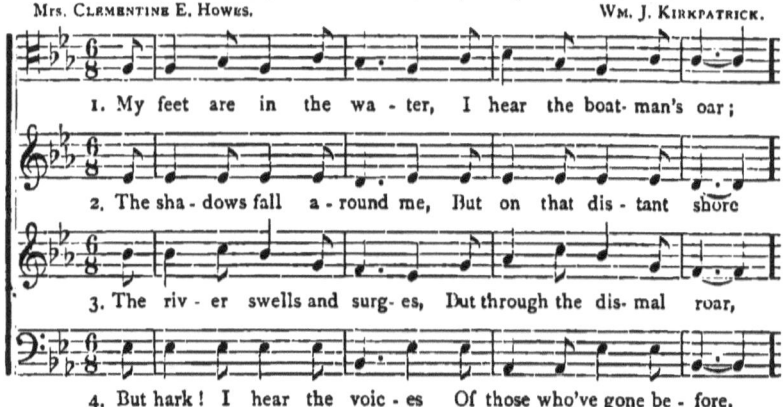

1. My feet are in the wa-ter, I hear the boat-man's oar;
2. The sha-dows fall a-round me, But on that dis-tant shore
3. The riv-er swells and surg-es, But through the dis-mal roar,
4. But hark! I hear the voic-es Of those who've gone be-fore,

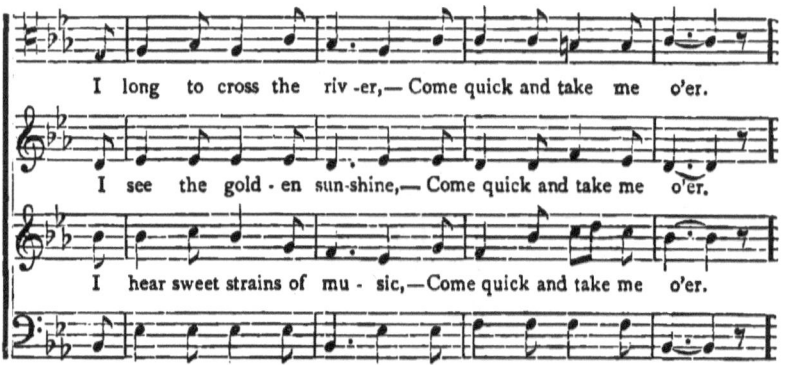

I long to cross the riv-er,—Come quick and take me o'er.
I see the gold-en sun-shine,—Come quick and take me o'er.
I hear sweet strains of mu-sic,—Come quick and take me o'er.
A sweet re-frain they're sing-ing, We've come to take thee o'er.

CHORUS.

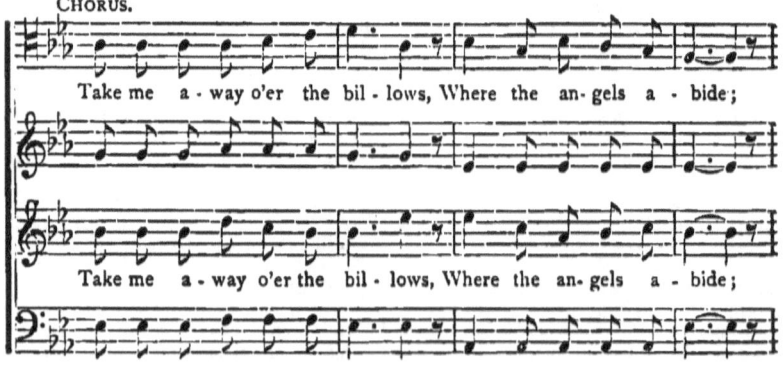

Take me a-way o'er the bil-lows, Where the an-gels a-bide;

Take me a-way o'er the bil-lows, Where the an-gels a-bide;

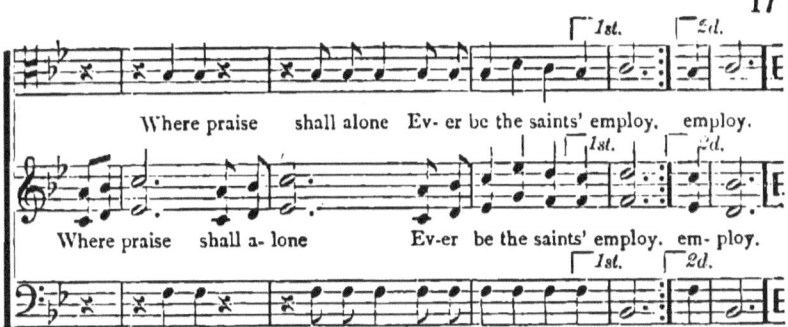

4 See now another mighty throng,
Un-numbered millions pass along
Into the realms of light;
All glory to the Saviour be,
It is the blood-washed company
Of saints arrayed in white!

5 All heaven resounds the glad refrain,
Worthy the Lamb for sinners slain!
They chant the victory:
Join the glad theme, haste the reply
O sinner, there may you and I
Begin eternity!

Endless Praise.

Rev. T. L. Baily.   Jno. R. Sweney.

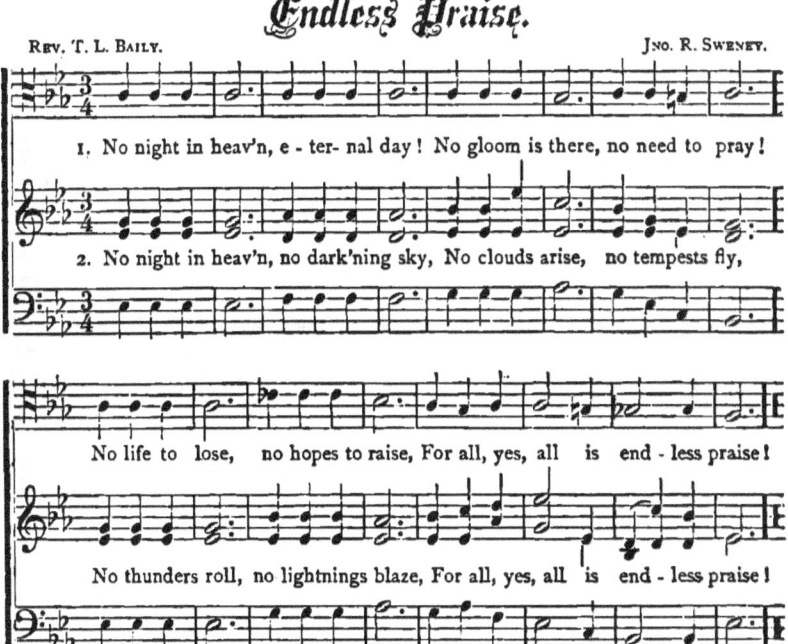

3 No night in heav'n, and yet no sun;
No morrow there her course to run!
No changing scenes to mark the days,
Where all, yes, all is endless praise!

B

4 No night in heav'n, God's light alone
In glory shines around the throne;
There to the Lamb, in joyous lays,
The hosts of heav'n give endless praise!

glow-ing bars and clust'ring stars, That have braved a hun-dred years!

glow-ing bars and clust'ring stars, That have braved a hun-dred years!

In Faithful Bonds United.

Arr. from BEETHOVEN.

1. In faithful bonds u-ni-ted By friendship's gentle pow'r, In social joys de-
2. When skies are bright above us, And sunshine cheers our way, When tender hearts that
3. So gloomy doubts and sadness Are chased afar by joy, And grateful songs of

light-ed, We spend the happy hour; No trouble o'er our plea-sure Its
love us, Grow fonder day by day; Each smile of kindness light-ens The
gladness Our hearts and tongues employ; While faithful-ly u-nit-ed By

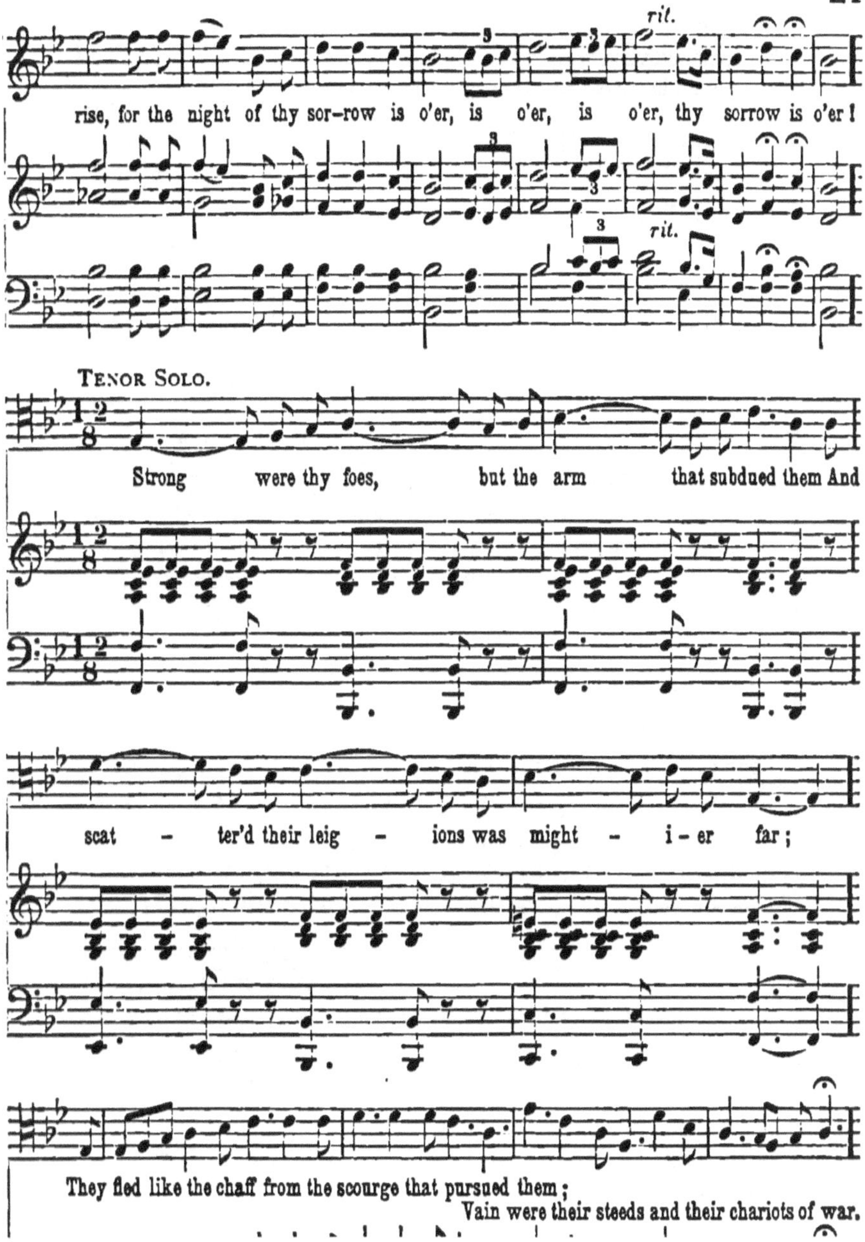
rit.
rise, for the night of thy sor-row is o'er, is o'er, is o'er, thy sorrow is o'er!
rit.
TENOR SOLO.
Strong were thy foes, but the arm that subdued them And
scat - ter'd their leig - ions was might - i - er far;
They fled like the chaff from the scourge that pursued them;
Vain were their steeds and their chariots of war.

Gather Life's Roses.

Mrs. L. S. Welch. Adam Geibel.

1. Gather the roses while you may, Whose summer of life is just begun; For
2. Gather life's roses while you may, For life at the best is but a span; With a
3. Gather the roses while you may, In work for the Master, work and pray; The

youth is only a summer's day; And flowers will fade in the noon-day sun; With your
willing mind, and a heart to pray; With a love to God, and a love to man, And
fields are white to the reaper's hand, The vineyards in purple glo- ry stand; Oh!

fresh, young hopes, and your hearts so gay, Ga - ther life's ro - ses
ea - ger hands for your life to - day, Ga - ther the ro - ses
bring your hearts to the work to - day,—Ga - ther life's ro - ses

while you may, Ga - ther life's ro - ses while you may.
rit.
while you may, Ga - ther the ro - ses while you may.
while you may, Ga - ther life's ro - ses while you may.

THE GARNER.

He will Gather the Wheat in His Garner.

HARRIET B. M'KEEVER.   JNO. R. SWENEY.

1. When Jesus shall gather the nations Before him at last to appear,
2. Shall we hear, from the lips of the Saviour, The words, 'Faithful servant, well done;'
3. He will smile when he looks on his children, And sees on the ransomed his seal;

Then, oh, how shall we stand in the judgment, When summoned our sentence to hear?
Or, trembling with fear and with anguish, Be banished away from his throne.
He will clothe them in heavenly beau-ty, As low at his footstool they kneel.

CHORUS.

He will gather the wheat in his gar-ner, But the chaff will he scatter a-way;

Then, oh, how shall we stand in the judgment Of the great Resurrection Day?

4 Then let us be watching and waiting,—
   Our lamps burning steady and bright,—
   When the Bridegroom shall call to the wed-
   Our spirits made ready for flight.   [ding

5 Thus living with hearts fixed on heaven,
   In patience we wait for the time,
   When, the days of our pilgrimage ended,
   We'll bask in the presence divine.

Are You Ready?

MARY D. JAMES.   JNO. R. SWENEY.

1. Should the summons, quickly fly - ing, On the slumb'ring nations fall,—
2. What if now the startling man - date Should the sleeping virgins hear,—
3. Is there oil in all your ves - sels? Are your garments pure and white?
4. Rise! ye virgins,—sleep no long - er,—Lest the call your souls sur - prise!

Lo! the Heav'nly Bridegroom com - eth, Would the sound your souls ap-pal?
Are your lamps all trimmed and burn-ing? Should the Bridegroom now appear?
Are they washed in-the cleansing Fountain, Fit to stand in Je - sus' sight?
Lest ye fail to meet the Bride - groom, When he cometh from the skies.

CHORUS.

Are you rea - dy?   Are you rea - dy?   Should you hear the midnight call?
Are you rea - dy?   Are you rea - dy?   Now to see your Lord appear!
Are you rea - dy?   Are you rea - dy?   Are your lamps all clear and bright?
Oh, be rea - dy!   Oh, be rea - dy!   When he cometh from the skies;

Are you rea - dy?   Are you rea - dy?   Should you hear the midnight call?
Are you rea - dy?   Are you rea - dy?   Now to see your Lord appear?
Are you rea - dy?   Are you rea - dy?   Are your lamps all clear and bright?
Oh, be rea - dy!   Oh, be rea - dy!   Hasten, from your slumbers rise!

Are you ready? Are you ready? Should you hear the midnight call? Should you hear the midnight call?
Are you ready? Are you ready? Now to see your Lord appear? Now to see your Lord ap- pear?
Are you ready? Are you ready? Are your lamps all clear and bright? Are your lamps all clear and bright?
Oh, be ready! Oh, be ready! Hasten, from your slumbers rise! Hasten, from your slumbers rise!

3 Anxious no longer for self,
  Shrinking no longer from pain;
  Leaning on Jesus alone,
  He all my care will sustain.
    Leaning on Jesus, etc.

4 Leaning, I walk in "The Way,"
  Leaning, "The Truth" I shall know;
  Leaning on heart-throbs of Christ,
  Safe into "Life" I may go.
    Leaning on Jesus, etc.

From "*Leaflet Gems, No. 2,*" by *per.*

No Love like the Love of Jesus.

W. J. Davies.

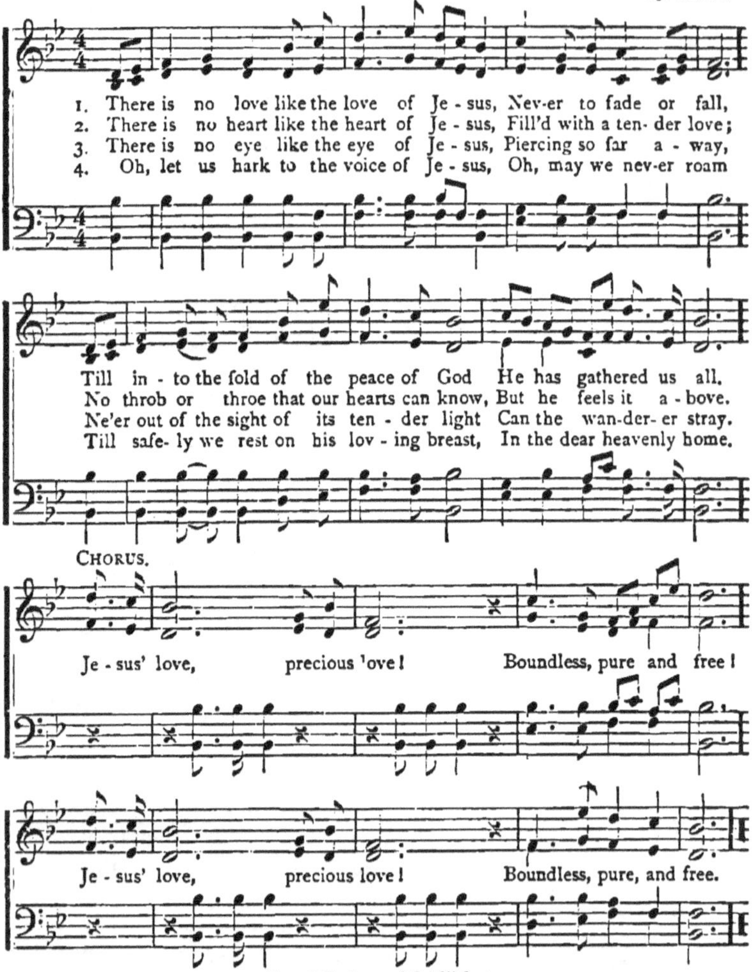

1. There is no love like the love of Je-sus, Nev-er to fade or fall,
2. There is no heart like the heart of Je-sus, Fill'd with a ten-der love;
3. There is no eye like the eye of Je-sus, Piercing so far a-way,
4. Oh, let us hark to the voice of Je-sus, Oh, may we nev-er roam

Till in-to the fold of the peace of God He has gathered us all.
No throb or throe that our hearts can know, But he feels it a-bove.
Ne'er out of the sight of its ten-der light Can the wan-der-er stray.
Till safe-ly we rest on his lov-ing breast, In the dear heavenly home.

CHORUS.

Je-sus' love, precious 'ove! Boundless, pure and free!

Je-sus' love, precious love! Boundless, pure, and free.

From "Jasper and Gold," by per.

JESUS, I MY CROSS HAVE TAKEN. Tune on page 29.

1 Jesus, I my cross have taken,
  All to leave and follow thee;
Naked, poor, despised, forsaken,
  Thou from hence my all shalt be!
Perish, every fond ambition,
  All I've sought, or hoped, or known,
Yet how rich is my condition;
  God and heaven are still my own!

2 Let the world despise and leave me,
  They have left my Saviour too;
Human hearts and looks deceive me,
  Thou art not like them untrue.
Oh, while thou dost smile upon me,
  God of wisdom, love and might,
Foes may hate, and friends disown me,
  Show thy face, and all is bright.

I'm a Pilgrim Going Home.

JNO. R. SWENEY.

1. Christians, I am on my journey, Ere I reach the nar-row sea, I would tell the wondrous sto-ry, What the Lord has done for me.
2. I was lost, but Je-sus found me, Taught my heart to seek his face; From a wild and lone-ly des-ert Brought me to his fold of grace.
3. Now my soul, with rapture glowing, Sings a-loud his pard'ning love; Looks be-yond a world of sor-row, To the pil-grim's home a-bove.
4. I shall yet be-hold my Saviour, When the day of life is o'er; I shall cast my crown be-fore him, I shall praise him ev-er-more.

D.S. *I am on my way to Zi-on, I'm a pil-grim go-ing home.*

CHORUS.

Glo-ry, glo-ry, hal-le-lu-jah! Though a stranger here I roam,

---

GLORIOUS THINGS OF THEE ARE SPOKEN.—8s & 7s, double.

TUNE.—"I'm a Pilgrim Going Home," without chorus.

1 Glorious things of thee are spoken,
  Zion, city of our God;
He whose word cannot be broken
  Formed thee for his own abode.
On the Rock of Ages founded,
  What can shake thy sure repose?
With salvation's walls surrounded,
  Thou may'st smile at all thy foes.

2 See the streams of living waters,
  Springing from eternal love,
Well supply thy sons and daughters,
  And all fear of want remove:

Who can faint while such a river
  Ever flows their thirst to-assuage,—
Grace which, like the Lord, the giver,
  Never fails from age to age?

3 Round each habitation hovering,
  See the cloud and fire appear,
For a glory and a covering,
  Showing that the Lord is near:
Thus deriving from the banner
  Light by night and shade by day,
Safe they feed upon the manna
  Which he gives them when they pray.

Rescue the Perishing.

FANNY H. CROSBY. W. H. DOANE.

1. Res-cue the per-ishing, Care for the dy-ing, Snatch them in pi-ty from sin and the grave; Weep o'er the err-ing one, Lift up the fall-en, Tell them of Je-sus the migh-ty to save. Res-cue the per-ishing, care for the dy-ing; Je-sus is mer-ci-ful, Je-sus will save.

2. Though they are slighting him, Still he is waiting, Wait-ing the pen-i-tent child to re-ceive, Plead with them ear-nest-ly, Plead with them gent-ly, He will for-give if they on-ly be-lieve.

3 Down in the human heart,
Crushed by the tempter,
Feelings lie buried that grace can restore:
Touched by a loving heart,
Wakened by kindness, [more.
Chords that were broken will vibrate once

4 Rescue the perishing,
Duty demands it;
Strength for thy labor the Lord will pro-
Back to the narrow way [vide:
Patiently win them;
Tell the poor wand'rer a Saviour has died.

From " Pure Gold," by per. of Messrs. Biglow & Main.

GO BURY THY SORROW.—Key B♭.

1 Go bury thy sorrow,
The world hath its share;
Go bury it deeply,
Go hide it with care,
Go think of it calmly,
When curtained by night,
Go tell it to Jesus,
And all will be right.

2 Go tell it to Jesus,
He knoweth thy grief;
Go tell it to Jesus,
He'll send thee relief;
Go gather the sunshine
He sheds on the way;
He'll lighten thy burden,
Go, weary one, pray,

3 Hearts growing a-weary
With heavier woe [ness,
Now droop 'mid the dark-
Go comfort them, go!
Go bury thy sorrows,
Let others be blest;
Go give them the sunshine,
Tell Jesus the rest.

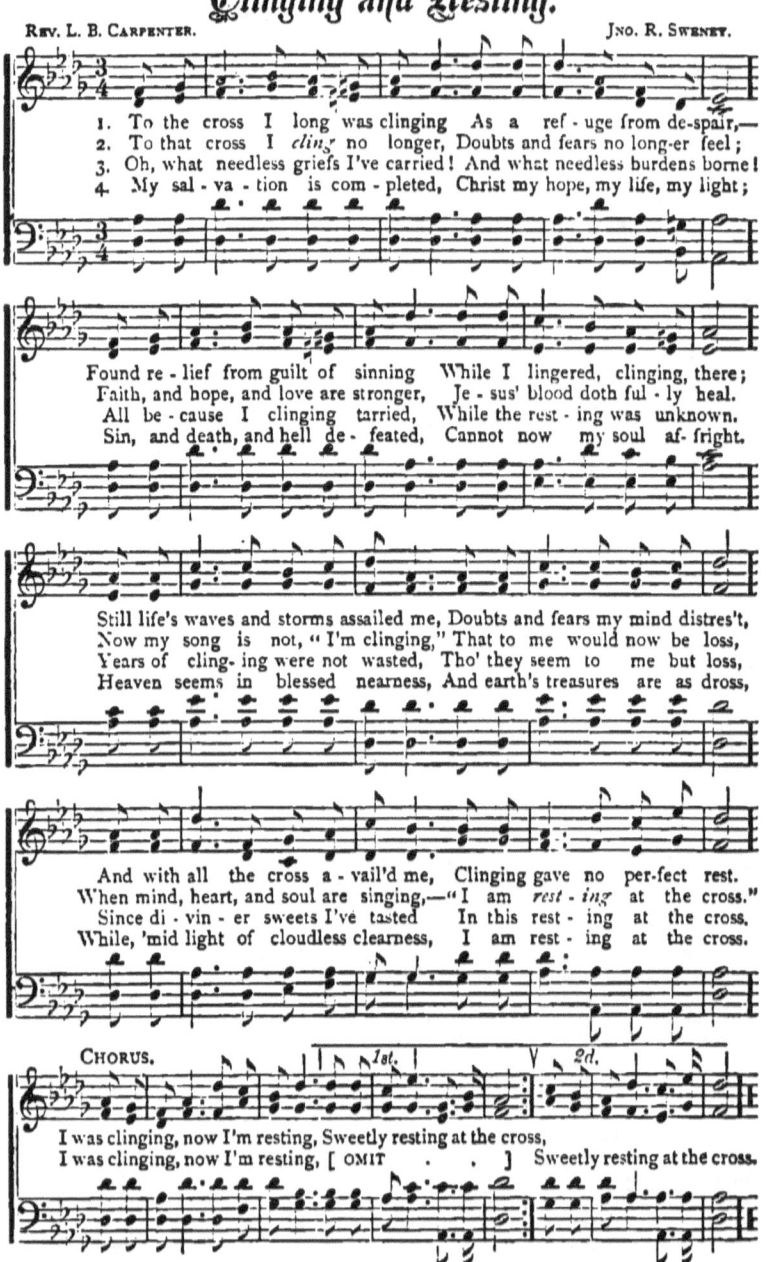

Joy Unknown. 33

J. H. JACKSON.   REV. J. H. STOCKTON.

1. A joy unknown to my poor soul The sweet as-surance gave, When Je-sus whispered, I am thine, And show'd his power to save: With new de-sires my heart o'er-flow'd, Nor could my lips re-frain, To tell the story of his love, And praise his wondrous name. Glory, glory to Je-sus!—

2. No darkness now, a glorious light Il-lum-ines all my way: Earth seems more glad, the skies more bright; I'm hap-py all the day: For Je-sus is my righteous-ness, He bore the guilt from me; His promised grace is all I need Forever his to be!

3. No more oppressed by guilty fears, From Satan's bondage free, I live a-lone for his dear sake, Who did so much for me. His love shall be my joy-ful theme, Through all my fleet-ing days, And when I stand before his throne New songs of love I'll raise.

CHORUS.

He is a-ble to save us; Glo-ry, glo-ry to Jesus! His blood avails for me.

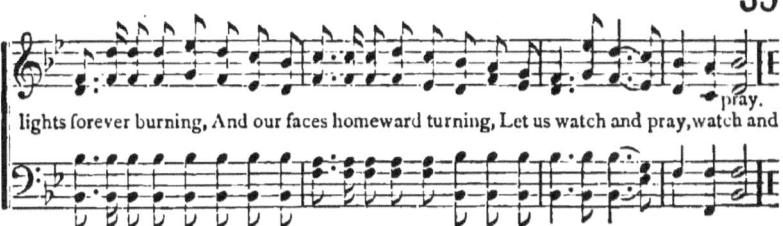

lights forever burning, And our faces homeward turning, Let us watch and pray, watch and pray.

Asbury Park. 7s.
FOR MALE VOICES.   Wm. G. Fischer.

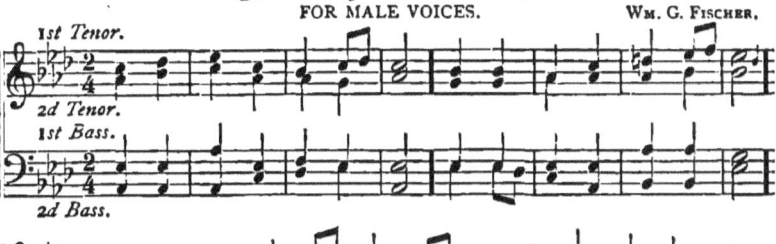

JESUS, LOVER OF MY SOUL. 7s.

1 Jesus, lover of my soul,
    Let me to thy bosom fly,
  While the nearer waters roll,
    While the tempest still is high;
  Hide me, O my Saviour, hide,
    Till the storm of life is past;
  Safe into the haven guide,
    O receive my soul at last.

2 Other refuge have I none;
    Hangs my helpless soul on thee:
  Leave, oh, leave me not alone,
    Still support and comfort me:
  All my trust on thee is stay'd,
    All my help from thee I bring;
  Cover my defenceless head
    With the shadow of thy wing.

3 Thou, O Christ, art all I want:
    More than all in thee I find:
  Raise the fallen, cheer the faint,
    Heal the sick, and lead the blind:
  Just and holy is thy name;
    I am all unrighteousness;
  False, and full of sin I am;
    Thou art full of truth and grace.

4 Plenteous grace with thee is found,
    Grace to cover all my sin;
  Let the healing streams abound;
    Make and keep me pure within.
  Thou of life the fountain art;
    Freely let me take of thee:
  Spring thou up within my heart;
    Rise to all eternity.

LORD, WE COME BEFORE THEE NOW. 7s.

1 Lord, we come before thee now,
    At thy feet we humbly bow;
  Oh, do not our suit disdain;
    Shall we seek thee, Lord, in vain?

2 Lord, on thee our souls depend;
    In compassion now descend;
  Fill our hearts with thy rich grace,
    Tune our lips to sing thy praise.

3 Send some message from thy word,
    That may joy and peace afford;
  Let thy Spirit now impart
    Full salvation to each heart.

4 Grant that all may seek and find
    Thee, a gracious God and kind;
  Heal the sick, the captive free;
    Let us all rejoice in thee.

36. Shall We Meet Beyond the River?

H. L. Hastings.   Elisha S. Rice.

1. Shall we meet beyond the riv-er, Where the surg-es cease to roll?
Where in all the bright for-ev-er, Sor-row ne'er shall press the soul?

2. Shall we meet in that blest harbor, When our storm-y voyage is o'er?
Shall we meet and cast the anchor By the bright ce-les-tial shore?

D.S. Shall we meet be-yond the riv-er, Where the surg-es cease to roll?

CHORUS.

Shall we meet, shall we meet, Shall we meet be-yond the riv-er?

3 Shall we meet in yonder city,
   Where the towers of crystal shine?
   Where the walls are all of jasper,
   Built by workmanship divine?

4 Where the music of the ransomed
   Rolls its harmony around,
   And creation swells the chorus
   With its sweet melodious sound?

5 Shall we meet there many a loved one,
   That was torn from our embrace?
   Shall we listen to their voices,
   And behold them face to face?

6 Shall we meet with Christ our Saviour,
   When he comes to claim his own?
   Shall we know his blessed favor,
   And sit down upon his throne?

From "New Silver Song," by permission.

Washed in the Blood of the Lamb. **

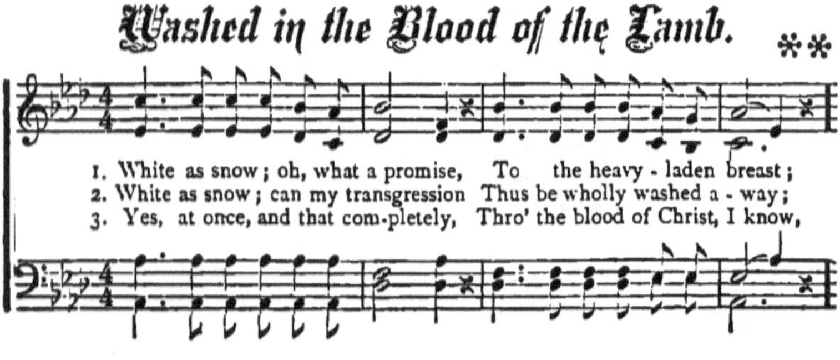

1. White as snow; oh, what a promise, To the heavy-laden breast;
2. White as snow; can my transgression Thus be wholly washed a-way;
3. Yes, at once, and that com-pletely, Thro' the blood of Christ, I know,

38. The River of Jordan.

"When thou passest through the waters, I will be with thee; and through the rivers, they shall not overflow thee."—Is. xliii. 2.

WM. E. BARBER.   JNO. R. SWENEY.

1. He came to the banks of the Jordan, But dreaded the wa-ters chill,
2. Still he stood on the banks of the Jordan, The Ci-ty of Gold in his view;
3. Then he linger'd no more by the Jordan, But plunged in the cold, dark flood,

Tho' his ear caught the whisper of promise, "Enter in, I'll be with thee still;
But the ice-cold waters deterred him, And he shrank from the passage through;
When he heard a great cho-rus of voices, Singing, "Saved by the Saviour's blood!

En-ter in, en-ter in, Without fear, without fear, For my
En-ter in, en-ter in, Without fear, without fear, For the
En-ter in, en-ter in, Without fear, without fear, To the

arms are beneath thee ev-er; On-ly trust, on-ly trust; Be of
riv-ers shall not o'er-flow thee; I have form'd, I've redeem'd, I have
king-dom prepared for you ev-er; No night, no sin here, No

cheer, good cheer, For my own I a-ban-don nev-er."
called thee by name, And as one of my own ones I know thee."
sick-ness, no tear, And the Lamb is the tem-ple for-ev-er."

So Much Like Jesus.

Rev. E. A. Hoffman.   T. C. O'Kane.

1. What is it that adorns the dai-ly life, And lights the face of them,
2. What is it that so richly crowns with grace, Like royal di-a-dem,
3. What is it sounding in their ev'ry tone, That seems to us so sweet?

Who journey onward in the path that leads To the New Je-ru-sa-lem?
The brow of those who travel in the way To the New Je-ru-sa-lem?
These virtues rare, they gather on-ly there, At the dear Redeemer's feet.

CHORUS.

They have been with Jesus, and have learned of him, He has wash'd them white as snow,

And they ev-er follow in the nar-row way, In his blessed paths they go.

From "Jasper and Gold," by per.

SHINING SHORE.   Key G.

1 My days are gliding swiftly by,
   And I, a pilgrim stranger,
Would not detain them as they fly:
   Those hours of toil and danger.
      CHORUS.
For oh! we stand on Jordan's strand,
   Our friends are passing over,
And just before, the shining shore
   We may almost discover.

2 We'll gird our loins, my brethren dear,
   Our distant home discerning;
Our absent Lord has left us word,
   Let every lamp be burning.

3 Let sorrow's rudest tempest blow,
   Each chord on earth to sever;
Our King says, Come, and there's our
   Forever, oh, forever!   [home,

We Shall Know.

Annie Herbert.   **J. H. Anderson.**

1. When the mists have roll'd in splendor From the beau-ty of the hills,
And the sun-shine, warm and tender, Falls in kiss-es on the rills,
We may read love's shining let-ter In the rain-bow of the spray,—
We shall know each oth-er bet-ter When the mists have cleared a-way.

2. If we err in hu-man blindness, And for-get that we are dust;
If we miss the law of kindness When we struggle to be just,
Snowy wings of peace shall cov-er All the plain that hides a-way,—
When the wea-ry watch is o-ver, And the mists have cleared a-way.

3. When the mists have risen a-bove us, As our Fa-ther knows his own,
Face to face with those that love us, We shall know as we are known;
Love, be-yond the o-rient meadows Floats the gold-en fringe of day,
Heart to heart, we bide the shadows, Till the mists have cleared a-way.

Chorus.

We shall know .. as we are known, .. Never more .. to walk a—
We shall know   as we are known,   Never-more

From "The Welcome," by per. of Messrs. S. Brainard's Sons.

Waiting for the Light.

Jno R. Sweney.

1. I am waiting, O my Father, For the coming of the light,—
2. I am waiting, bless-ed Saviour, Let thy presence light my way,
3. I am waiting, Lord, why tarry? En-ter quick the open door,
4. I am waiting, O my Father, Yet I see the coming light,

For the sun-shine of thy presence, That shall lift the clouds of night.
Let thy loving hand e'er lead me, Let me nev-er from thee stray.
Let me feel that thou art with me, And I ask for nothing more.
Yet I feel thy ten-der presence, Nev-er more shall it be night.

CHORUS.
I am waiting for thy foot-step, As it comes toward my door;—
I am waiting, I am waiting for thy footstep, As it comes, yes, as it comes toward my door;

rall.
O, my Father, en-ter quickly, Leave me never, never more.

ONLY TRUST HIM.—Key G.

1 Come, every soul by sin oppressed,
There's mercy with the Lord,
And he will surely give you rest,
By trusting in his word.
CHORUS.
Only trust him, only trust him,
Only trust him now;
He will save you, he will save you,
He will save you now.

2 For Jesus shed his precious blood
Rich blessings to bestow;
Plunge now into the crimson tide
That washes white as snow.

3 Yes, Jesus is the Truth, the Way,
That leads you into rest;
Believe in him without delay,
And you are fully blest.

The New Jerusalem.

"Our feet shall stand within thy gates, O Jerusalem."

Rev. Wm. H. Hunter, D. D. Jno. R. Sweney.

1. Je-ru-sa-lem! thy mansions fair Ig-noble souls may never share;
   For all who walk thy streets of gold Are in the book of life en-roll'd.
2. Who-so from earth would thither go, Must wash his robes as white as snow;—
   In Je-sus' blood, the fount of grace, Find pure, unspotted righteousness.

Chorus.

O, Je-ru-sa-lem! O, Je-ru-sa-lem! Our feet with-in thy gates shall stand! O, Je-ru-sa-lem! New Je-ru-sa-lem!

3 O Lamb of God, my heart prepare,
To enter with the holy there;
Within thy book my name enroll,
And write thine own upon my soul.

4 To him that loves and trusts the Lord,
And keeps with patient hope his word,
The Spirit with his spirit bears
Sweet witness to his answered prayers.

5 Whoever has this seal of love
His title reads to seats above;
And looking upward as he runs,
The taint of sinful pleasure shuns.

6 Jesus, fulfil my long desire
To stand with thee in pure attire,
And find at last a place and name
Within the New Jerusalem.

Copyright, 1877, by JOHN J. HOOD.

The Smitten Rock.

45

"Thou shalt smite the rock, and there shall come water out of it, that the people may drink." Ex. xvii.
"They drank of that spiritual rock that followed them, and that rock was Christ."—1 Cor. x. 4.

GEO. C. NEEDHAM.   IRA D. SANKEY. By per.

1. From the riv-en Rock there floweth Liv-ing wa-ter, ev-er clear;
2. "Without money, with-out mer-it," Je-sus calls, "Come unto me,"
3. Fainting in the des-ert, dreary, Guil-ty sin-ner, hark! 'tis He!

Wea-ry pil-grim, journeying onward, Know you not that Fount is near?
Thirsty traveller, be en-couraged, Know you not the Fount is free?
'Tis the Saviour still en-treating, Know you not he call-eth thee?

CHORUS.

Je-sus is the Rock of A-ges—Smitten, stricken, lo! he dies;
From his side a liv-ing fountain, Know you not it sat-is-fies?

WHAT HAST THOU DONE FOR ME? Key C.

1 I gave my life for thee,
  My precious blood I shed,
That thou might'st ransomed be,
  And quickened from the dead;
I gave, I gave my life for thee,
What hast thou given for me?

2 My Father's house of light,
  My glory-circled throne
I left, for earthly night,
  For wand'rings sad and lone;
I left, I left it all for thee,
Hast thou left aught for me?

3 I suffered much for thee,
  More than thy tongue can tell,
Of bitterest agony,
  To rescue thee from hell;
I've borne, I've borne it all for thee,
What hast thou borne for me?

4 And I have brought to thee,
  Down from my home above,
Salvation full and free,
  My pardon and my love;
I bring, I bring rich gifts to thee,
What hast thou brought to me?

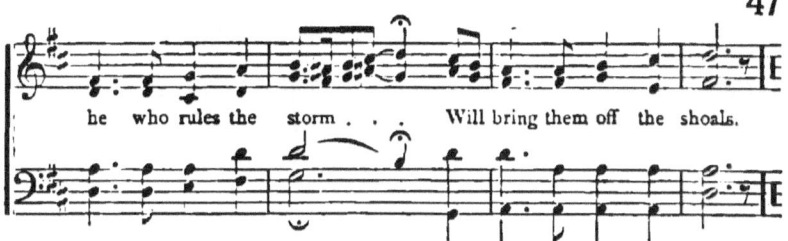

he who rules the storm . . . Will bring them off the shoals.

Why not To-night?

Anon.   J. S. H.

Oh! do not let the Word depart, Nor close thine eyes against the Light,

Poor sinner, harden not your heart, Thou would'st be saved, why not to-night?

REFRAIN.   Rit.

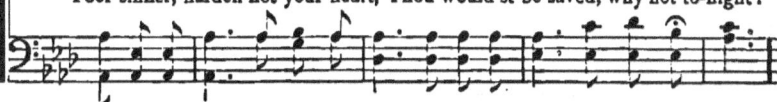

Why not to-night? why not to-night? Thou would'st be saved, why not to-night?

2 To-morrow's sun may never rise
   To bless thy long-deluded sight,
   This is the time, oh, then, be wise!
     Thou would'st be saved, why not to-
       night?

3 Our God in pity lingers still,
   And wilt thou thus his love requite?
   Renounce at length thy stubborn will,
     Thou would'st be saved, why not to-
       night?

4 The world has nothing left to give,
   It has no new, no pure delight;
   Oh, try the life which Christians live,
     Thou would'st be saved, why not to-
       night?

5 Our blessed Lord refuses none
   Who would to him their souls unite,
   Then be the work of grace begun,
     Thou would'st be saved, why not to-
       night?

Jesus, Love Me Still.

Rev. E. A. Hoffman. Jno. R. Sweney.

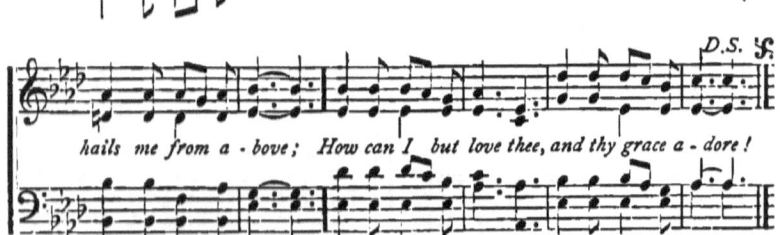

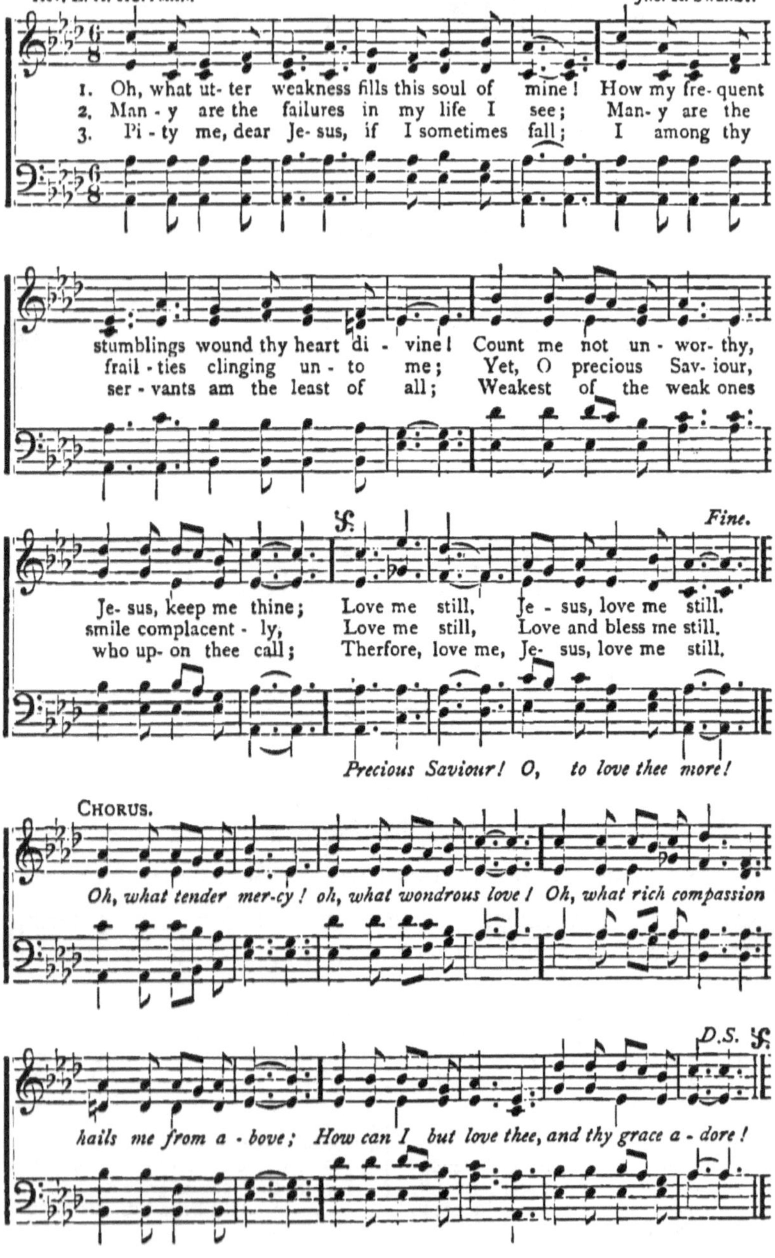

Tender Shepherd.

Words arr., and Melody by the late Rev. J. H. Stockton. Har. by Wm. J. Kirkpatrick.

Tenderly, with expression.

1. Ten-der Shepherd, Help me, Save me, I have wandered Far a-way;
   I am help-less, sick, and dy-ing; Wilt thou not take me Back to-day?

2. Ten-der Shepherd, Lead me, Feed me, Or I famish By the way,
   For I faint for heavenly man-na, And I need it Day by day.

CHORUS.

O thou ten-der Shepherd, I've wander'd far a-way from thee;
Take me back, loving Shepherd; Is there not room in thy fold for me?

3 Tender Shepherd
    Watch me,
    Guide me;
Rough and dark I find the way,
And I need thee close beside me;
    For I wander
    Day by day.

4 Tender Shepherd,
    Take me,
    Keep me
When I lay me down to die;
For I'm lost, unless the Shepherd
    Takes me to the
    Fold on high.

D

Deliverance will Come.

Words arr.   Arr. by Rev. W. M'Donald. By per.

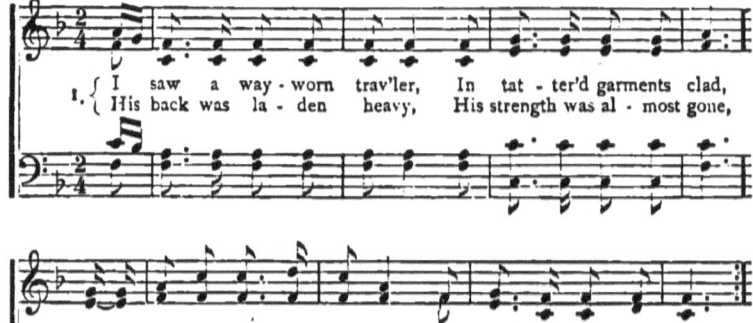

1. I saw a way-worn trav'ler, In tatter'd garments clad,
   His back was laden heavy, His strength was almost gone,
   And struggling up the mountain, It seemed that he was sad;
   Yet he shouted as he journey'd, Deliverance will come.

CHORUS.

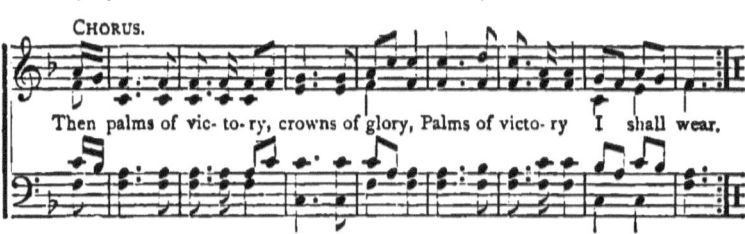

Then palms of victory, crowns of glory, Palms of victory I shall wear.

2 The summer sun was shining,
   The sweat was on his brow,
   His garments worn and dusty,
   His step seemed very slow :
   But he kept pressing onward,
   For he was wending home ;
   Still shouting as he journeyed,
   Deliverance will come!

3 The songsters in the arbor
   That stood beside the way
   Attracted his attention,
   Inviting his delay:
   His watchword being "Onward!"
   He stopped his ears and ran,
   Still shouting as he journeyed,
   Deliverance will come!

4 I saw him in the evening,
   The sun was bending low,
   He'd overtopped the mountain
   And reached the vale below:
   He saw the golden city,—
   His everlasting home,—
   And shouted loud, Hosanna,
   Deliverance will come!

5 While gazing on that city,
   Just o'er the narrow flood,
   A band of holy angels
   Came from the throne of God :
   They bore him on their pinions
   Safe o'er the dashing foam,
   And joined him in his triumph,—
   Deliverance has come!

6 I heard the song of triumph
   They sang upon that shore,
   Saying, Jesus has redeemed us
   To suffer nevermore:
   Then, casting his eyes backward
   On the race which he had run,
   He shouted loud, Hosanna,
   Deliverance has come!

The Invitation.

Whosoever will, let him come and take of the water of life freely.

R. KELSO CARTER.   JNO. R. SWENEY.

1. Come! for the invitation Is urgent, boundless, free, And Christ, our blessed Saviour, Is calling now to thee; Come in youth's cloudless morning, When brightest hopes engage; Come in full manhood's glory, Come in the snows of age. Delay not for to-morrow, Oh,

Cho. to last verse, Delay not till to-morrow, Oh,

CHORUS.

wanderer, come home, To-day the voice of Jesus Is call- ing thee, oh, come.
wand'rer, do not wait, Delay not, for to-morrow May be one day too late.

2 Come listen to the story,
  So old, and yet so new,
How death and hell were vanquished,
  When Jesus died for you;
For you with thorns they crowned him,
For you they pierced his side,
Come, for the stream is flowing
  For you, so deep and wide.
    Delay not, etc.

3 Turn from the path of evil,
  The way of life is free;
Come! for the door is open,
  Stands open wide for thee;
Come! all who sit in darkness,
  Come! all by sin oppressed,
Come! weary, heavy-laden,
  And I will give you rest.
    Delay not, etc.

To tell the old, old sto - ry, Of Je - sus and his love.

3 I love to tell the story!
'Tis pleasant to repeat
What seems, each time I tell it,
More wonderfully sweet.
I love to tell the story;
For some have never heard
The message of salvation
From God's own Holy Word.

4 I love to tell the story!
For those who know it best
Seem hungering and thirsting
To hear it like the rest.
And when, in scenes of glory,
I sing the *New, New Song,*
'Twill be the *Old, Old Story,*
That I have loved so long.

Mrs. E. Codner.

Even Me.

Jno. R. Sweney.

1. Lord, I hear of showers of blessing, Thou art scatt'ring full and free—
Showers, the thirst-y land re-freshing; Let some droppings fall on me.—
E - ven me, Yes, e - ven me, E - ven me, yes, e - ven me.—

2. Pass me not, O gracious Father! Sin - ful tho' my heart may be;
Thou might'st leave me, but the rath- er Let thy mer - cy fall on me.—

3. Pass me not, O ten- der Saviour! Let me live and cling to thee;
I am long - ing for thy fa- vor; Whilst thou'rt calling, oh, call me.—

4 Pass me not, O mighty Spirit!
Thou can'st make the blind to see;
Witnesser of Jesus' merit,
Speak the word of power to me,—
Even me, even me, etc.

5 Love of God, so pure and changeless;
Blood of Christ, so rich and free;
Grace of God, so strong and boundless;
Magnify them all in me,—
Even me, even me, etc.

5 Dear Jesus, for this I most humbly entreat;
I wait, blessed Lord, at thy crucified feet;
By faith, for my cleansing, I see thy blood flow,—
Now wash me, and I shall be whiter than snow.

6 The blessing by faith I receive from above;
O glory! my soul is made perfect in love;
My prayer has prevailed, and this moment I know
The blood is applied,—I am whiter than snow.

I've been Redeemed.

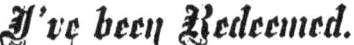

Plantation Melody. Arr. by Dr. T. H. Peacock. By per.

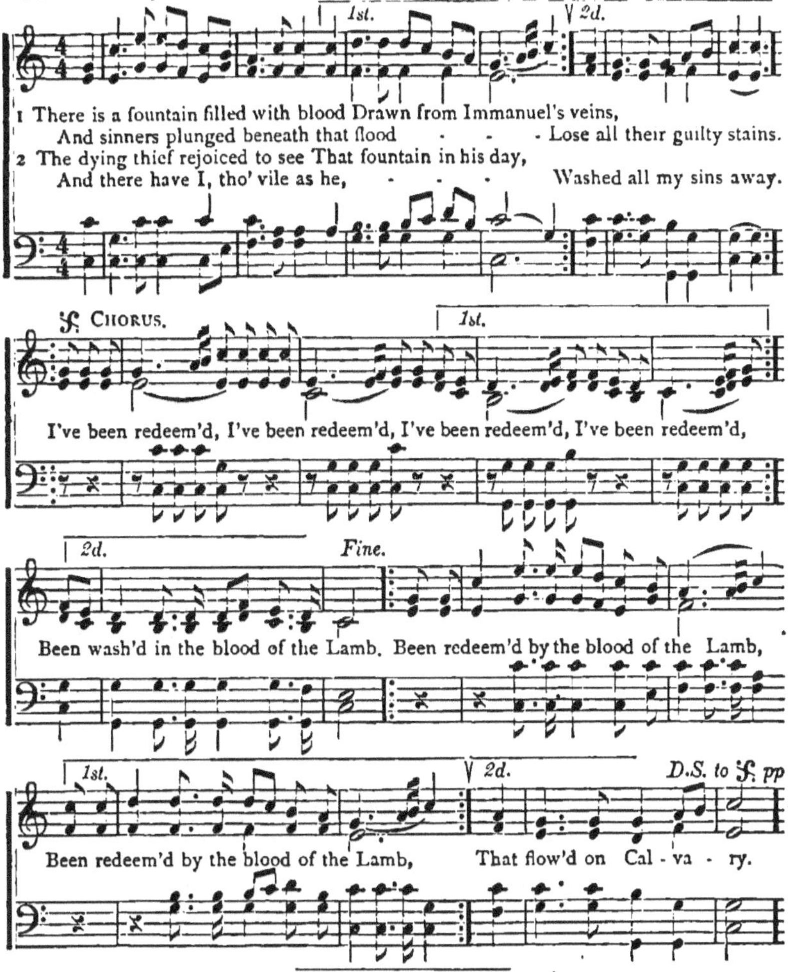
1st.
2d.
1 There is a fountain filled with blood Drawn from Immanuel's veins,
And sinners plunged beneath that flood - - - Lose all their guilty stains.
2 The dying thief rejoiced to see That fountain in his day,
And there have I, tho' vile as he, - - - Washed all my sins away.
CHORUS.
1st.
I've been redeem'd, I've been redeem'd, I've been redeem'd, I've been redeem'd,
2d.
Fine.
Been wash'd in the blood of the Lamb. Been redeem'd by the blood of the Lamb,
1st.
2d.
D.S. to 𝄋 pp
Been redeem'd by the blood of the Lamb, That flow'd on Cal - va - ry.

ALL TO CHRIST I OWE.—Key E♭.

1 I hear the Saviour say,
Thy strength indeed is small;
Child of weakness, watch and pray,
Find in me thine all in all.

Cho.—*Jesus paid it all,*
All to him I owe;
Sin had left a crimson stain,
He washed it white as snow.

2 Lord, now indeed I find
Thy power, and thine alone,
Can change the leper's spots,
And melt the heart of stone.

3 For nothing good have I
Whereby thy grace to claim,—
I'll wash my garment white
In the blood of Calvary's Lamb.

4 When from my dying bed
My ransomed soul shall rise,
Then "Jesus paid it all"
Shall rend the vaulted skies.

5 And when before the throne
I stand in him complete,
I'll lay my trophies down,
All down at Jesus' feet.

Believing.*

C. WESLEY. REV. J. H. STOCKTON.

1. Jesus, thine all victorious love Shed in my heart abroad;
Then shall my feet no longer rove, Rooted and fixed in God.

CHORUS.
I'm be-liev-ing, I'm be-liev-ing, Believing now in the Lord;
I'm be-liev-ing, and re-ceiv-ing Salvation through his blood.

2 O that in me the sacred fire
Might now begin to glow;
Burn up the dross of base desire,
And make the mountains flow.

3 O that it now from heaven might fall,
And all my sins consume:
Come, Holy Ghost, for thee I call;
Spirit of burning, come.

4 Refining fire, go through my heart:
Illuminate my soul;
Scatter thy life in every part,
And sanctify the whole.

5 My steadfast soul, from falling free,
Shall then no longer move;
While Christ is all the world to me,
And all my heart is love.

ALAS! AND DID MY SAVIOUR BLEED? C. M.

1 Alas! and did my Saviour bleed?
And did my Sov'reign die?
Would he devote that sacred head
For such a worm as I?
CHORUS.
Help me, dear Saviour, thee to own,
And ever faithful be;
And when thou sittest on thy throne,
O Lord, remember me.

2 Was it for crimes that I have done
He groaned upon the tree!
Amazing pity! grace unknown!
And love beyond degree!

3 Well might the sun in darkness hide,
And shut his glories in,
When Christ, the mighty Maker, died
For man, the creature,'s sin.

4 Thus might I hide my blushing face
While his dear cross appears;
Dissolve my heart in thankfulness,
And melt mine eyes to tears.

5 But drops of grief can ne'er repay
The debt of love I owe:
Here, Lord, I give myself away,—
'Tis all that I can do.

* From "Precious Songs," by per.

I'll Enter the Open Door.

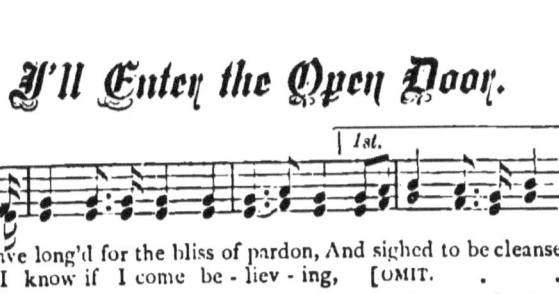

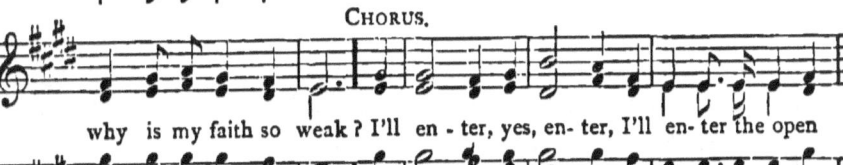

2 I will trust, tho' I walk in darkness,
   And pray till the light I see;
For the blood that can cleanse the vilest
   Will surely avail for me:
I have only this plea to offer,
   That Jesus for me has died;
And, with only my heart to give him,
   I haste to his blessed side.

3 I have long'd for the bliss of pardon,
   And sighed to be free from sin,
And I knock at the door, believing
   That Jesus will let me in:
Oh, the faith in my heart grows stronger,
   I tremble with fear no more;
'Tis my Saviour that bids me welcome,
   I'll enter the open door.

Storm the Fort.

Now shall the prince of this world be cast out.—John xii. 31.

REV. J. B. VINTON.   JNO. R. SWENEY.

1. Ho! my comrades, see the sig-nal Je-sus waves on high! Satan's bat-tle-ments are reel-ing, Hear our Captain's cry: "Storm the fort, for I am leading; I have shown you how;" Shout the an-swer back to heav-en, "We are ready,— *now!*"
2. See! the lof-ty walls are frowning, Held by Sa-tan's power; Sin enshrouds the world in darkness, Now's the storming hour.
3. See! the prophets now are showing How the fort must fall; There is no such thing as fail-ing, Shout, my comrades, all!
4. Fierce and long the siege has last-ed, But the end is near; On-ward leads our great Com-mander, Cheer, my comrades, cheer!

CHORUS.

SHALL WE GATHER AT THE RIVER.—Key E♭.

1 Shall we gather at the river,
  Where bright angel-feet have trod?
  With its crystal tide forever
  Flowing by the throne of God?
      CHORUS.
  Yes, we'll gather at the river,
    The beautiful, the beautiful river,
  Gather with the saints at the river
    That flows by the throne of God.

2 Ere we reach the shining river
  Lay we every burden down,
  Grace our spirits will deliver,
  And provide a robe and crown.

3 Soon we'll reach the shining river,
  Soon our pilgrimage will cease,
  Soon our happy hearts will quiver
  With the melody of peace.

Used by permission of Rev. R. Lowry.

3 If we knew the baby fingers,
   Pressed against the window-pane,
   Would be cold and stiff to-morrow,—
   Never trouble us again,—
   Would the bright eyes of our darling
   Catch the frown upon our brow?—
   Would the prints of rosy fingers
   Vex us then as they do now?

4 Ah! those little ice-cold fingers,
   How they point the memories back
   To the hasty words and actions
   Strewn around our backward track!
   How these little hands remind us,
   As in snowy grace they lie,
   Not to scatter thorns, but roses,
   For our reaping by and by.

Take Me as I Am.

Melody by the late Rev. J. H. Stockton. Har. by W. J. K.

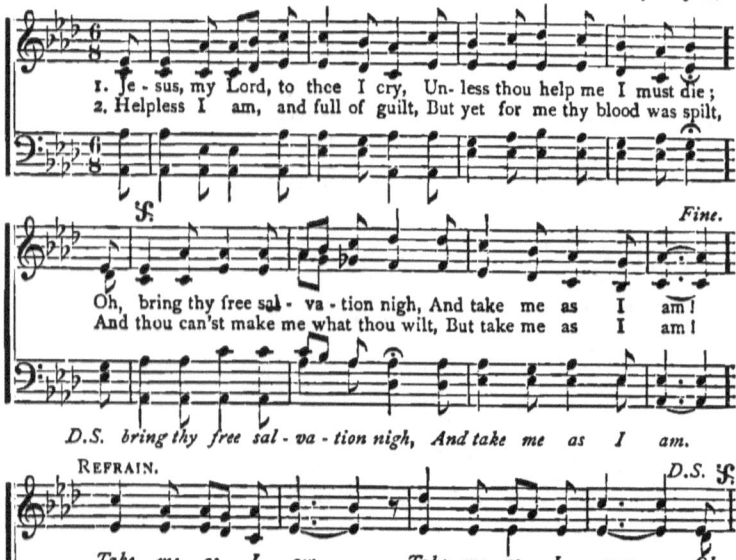

1. Je-sus, my Lord, to thee I cry, Un-less thou help me I must die;
2. Helpless I am, and full of guilt, But yet for me thy blood was spilt,

Oh, bring thy free sal-va-tion nigh, And take me as I am!
And thou can'st make me what thou wilt, But take me as I am!

D.S. bring thy free sal-va-tion nigh, And take me as I am.

REFRAIN.

Take me as I am, Take me as I am; Oh,
take me as I am, take me as I am;

3 No preparation can I make,
  My best resolves I only break,
  Yet save me for thine own name's sake,
  And take me as I am!

4 I thirst, I long to know thy love,
  Thy full salvation I would prove;
  But since to thee I cannot move,
  Oh, take me as I am!

5 If thou hast work for me to do,
  Inspire my will, my heart renew,
  And work both in and by me too,
  But take me as I am!

6 And when at last the work is done,
  The battle o'er, the vict'ry won,
  Still, still my cry shall be alone,
  Lord, take me as I am!

JUST AS I AM.—Tune and Chorus above.

1 Just as I am, without one plea,
  But that thy blood was shed for me,
  And that thou bid'st me come to thee,
    O Lamb of God, I come!

2 Just as I am, and waiting not
  To rid my soul of one dark blot, [spot,
  To thee, whose blood can cleanse each
    O Lamb of God, I come!

3 Just as I am, though tossed about
  With many a conflict, many a doubt,
  Fightings within, and fears without,
    O Lamb of God, I come!

4 Just as I am, poor, wretched, blind,
  Sight, riches, healing of the mind,
  Yea, all I need in thee to find,
    O Lamb of God, I come!

5 Just as I am, thou wilt receive,
  Wilt welcome, pardon, cleanse, relieve;
  Because thy promise I believe,
    O Lamb of God, I come!

6 Just as I am, thy love unknown
  Hath broken every barrier down;
  Now, to be thine, and thine alone,
    O Lamb of God, I come!

I Love to Trust in Jesus.

MARY D. JAMES. *In thee, O Lord, do I put my trust.*—Ps. 31, 1. JNO. R. SWENEY.

1. I love to trust in Jesus,—My Saviour, so adored,—
A solid Rock beneath my feet Is his unfailing Word.
I know this firm foundation, And feel I'm so secure!
His precious word is tried and prov'd, His promises are sure!

2 When arms of flesh are failing,
And earth seems cold and drear,
I love to trust in his strong arm,—
For then he draws so near!
In deepest midnight darkness,
When not a star I see,
The harder then I lean on him,
For then he's nearest me.

3 And when the raging billows
Are threatening to o'erwhelm,
I love to trust in Jesus then,
For he is at the helm!
Though clouds obscure his presence,
I know he's just as near,
And still I trust his changeless love,
And will not yield to fear.

4 I love to trust in Jesus,—
In life's bewildering maze,
When not one step ahead I see
In all the devious ways,
For well I know he leads me,
I feel his mighty hand
Is holding mine, each step I take
Through all this hostile land.

5 And when, in life's last conflict,
My heart and flesh shall fail,
When o'er this frail mortality
The last foe shall prevail,
Oh, then I'll trust in Jesus !—
The glorious, conquering King !—
Who vanquished the destroyer Death,
And took away his sting.

Copyright, 1878, by JOHN J. HOOD.

66. Not Knowing.

Ar from a poem by Miss M. G. Brainard.
My times are in thy hand.—Ps. 31, 15.
Jno. R. Sweney.

Con espressione.

1. I know not what shall befall me, God hangs a mist o'er my eyes,
And at each step in my onward way, He makes new scenes to arise,
And ev'ry joy he sends to me Is a strange and sweet surprise,

CHORUS.
Not knowing, not knowing, I'll follow Jesus my Saviour, Not knowing, not knowing, I'll follow where'er he leads.

2 I see not a step before me,
As I tread { the passing / on another } year,
The past is still in God's keeping,
The future his mercy will clear,
And what looks dark in the distance
May brighten as I draw near.

3 It may be he keeps, waiting
The coming of my feet,
Some gift of such rare beauty,
Some joy so strangely sweet,
That my lips shall only tremble
With the thanks they cannot speak.

4th and 5th verses at foot of opposite page.

Copyright, 1878, by JOHN J. HOOD.

The Land Just Across the River.

T. C. O'Kane. By per.

1. On Jordan's stormy banks I stand, And cast a wishful eye
2. O'er all these wide-extended plains Shines one eternal day;
3. When shall I reach that happy place, And be forever blest?
4. Filled with delight, my raptured soul Would here no longer stay;

To Canaan's fair and happy land, Where my possessions lie.
There God the Son forever reigns, And scatters night away.
When shall I see my Father's face, And in his bosom rest?
Tho' Jordan's waves around me roll, Fearless I'd launch away.

CHORUS.

We will rest in the fair and happy land, Just across on the evergreen shore, ..
by and by, evergreen shore.

Sing the song of Moses and the Lamb, by and by, And dwell with Jesus evermore.

NOT KNOWING.—*Continued from opposite page.*

4 Oh, restful, blissful darkness!
   'Tis blessed not to know,—
It keeps me still in the arms of God,
   Which will not let me go;
My soul is hushed to peaceful rest
   In the heart that loves me so.

5 So I go onward, not knowing,
   I would not if I might,—
I'd rather walk in the dark with God
   Than walk alone in the light,—
I'd rather walk with him by faith
   Than walk alone by sight.

2 O why is thine apparel
  With reeking gore all dyed,
Like them that tread the winepress red?
  O why this bloody tide?
    "I the winepress trod alone,
      'Neath darkening skies;
    Of the people there was none
      Mighty to save."

3 O bleeding Lamb, my Saviour,
    How couldst thou bear this shame?
  "With mercy fraught, mine own arm
    Salvation in my name;   [brought
    I the bloody fight have won,
      Conquered the grave,
    Now the year of joy has come,—
      Mighty to save."

The Saviour at the Door.

EDGAR PAGE.   JNO. R. SWINEY.

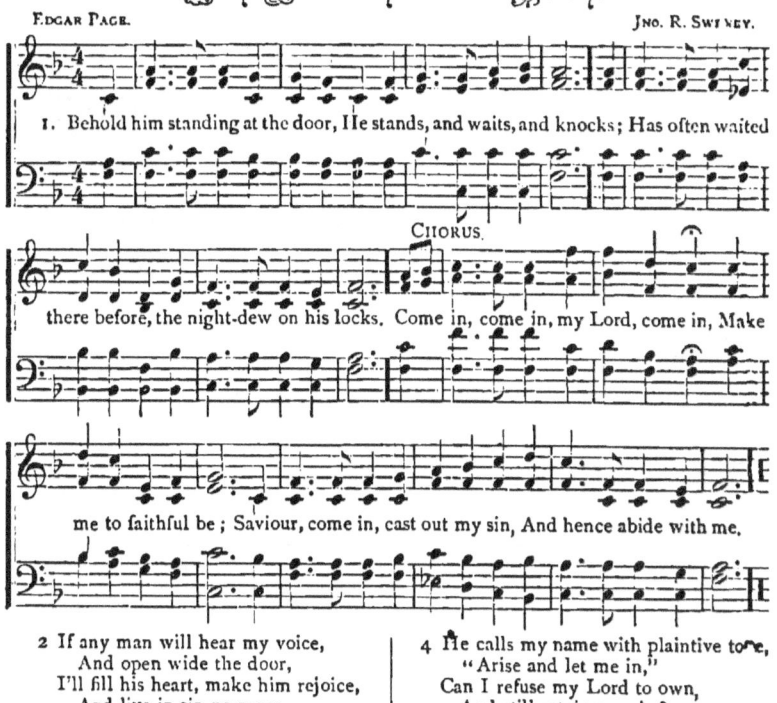

1. Behold him standing at the door, He stands, and waits, and knocks; Has often waited there before, the night-dew on his locks. Come in, come in, my Lord, come in, Make me to faithful be; Saviour, come in, cast out my sin, And hence abide with me.

2 If any man will hear my voice,
    And open wide the door,
  I'll fill his heart, make him rejoice,
    And live in sin no more.

3 I'll enter in to him and make
    A feast of joy and love,
  Like unto that the angels take
    In Father's house above.

4 He calls my name with plaintive tone,
    "Arise and let me in,"
  Can I refuse my Lord to own,
    And still retain my sin?

5 Saviour, I cannot shut thee out,
    Come, Lord, within my heart;
  Come, and remove my every doubt,
    Nor from me e'er depart.

HOME OF THE SOUL. Key E♭.

1 I will sing you a song of a beautiful land,
    The far-away home of the soul,
  Where no storms ever beat on the glittering strand,
    While the years of eternity roll. etc.

2 Oh, that home of the soul in my visions and dreams,
    Its bright, jasper walls I can see;
  Till I fancy but thinly the veil intervenes
    Between the fair city and me. etc.

3 That unchangeable home is for you and for me,
    Where Jesus of Nazareth stands;
  The King of all kingdoms forever is he,
    And he holdeth our crowns in his hands. etc.

4 Oh, how sweet it will be in that beautiful land,
    So free from all sorrow and pain,
  With songs on our lips, and with harps in our hands,
    To meet one another again. etc.

The Golden Key.

"Prayer is the key to unlock the day, and the bolt to shut in the night."

Jno. R. Sweney.

1. Prayer is the key For the bending knee To open the morn's first hours;
2. Not a soul so sad, Nor a heart so glad, When cometh the shades of night,

See the incense rise To the star-ry skies, Like per-fume from the flow'rs.
But the daybreak song Will the joy prolong, And some darkness turn to light.

3 Take the golden key
In your hand, and see,
As the night-tide drifts away,
How its blessed hold
Is a crown of gold,
Thro' the weary hours of day.

4 When the shadows fall,
And the vesper call
Is sobbing its low refrain,
'Tis a garland sweet
To the toil-dent feet,
And an antidote for pain.

5 Soon the year's dark door
Shall be shut no more;
Life's tears shall be wiped away
As the pearl-gates swing,
And the gold harps ring,
And the sun unsheathe for aye.

From "Goodly Pearls," by per.

The Watchman's Cry.

FOR MIXED VOICES.

W. B. Evans.

1. Hark! 'tis the watchman's cry,—Wake, brethren, wake! Jesus our Lord is nigh, Wake, brethren, wake!

Sleep is for sons of night; Children are ye of light; Yours is the glory bright; Wake, brethren, wake!

Other verses on opposite page.

The Watchman's Cry.

FOR MALE VOICES.   WM. J. KIRKPATRICK.

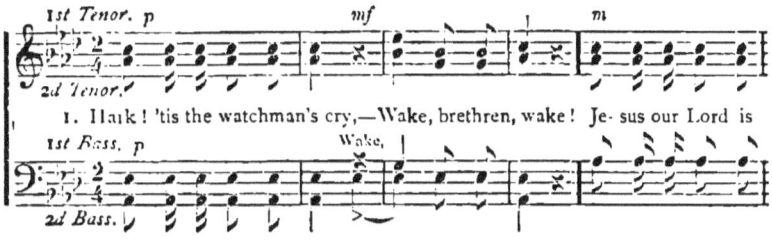
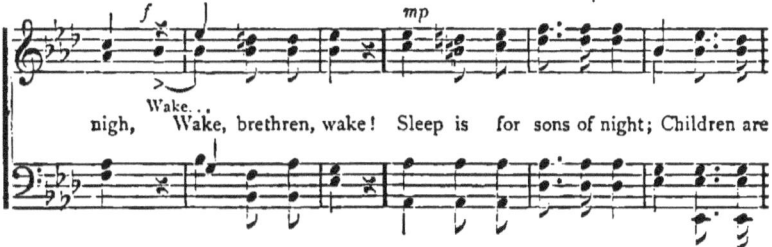
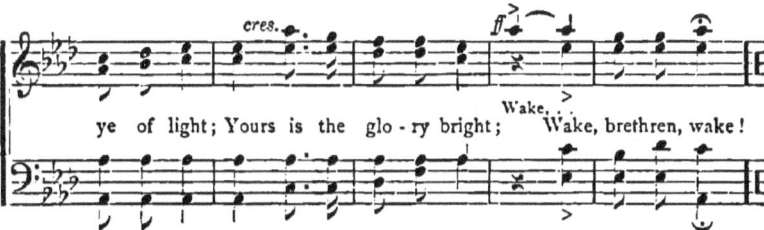

2 Call to each working band,
   Watch, brethren, watch!
  Clear is our Lord's command,
   Watch, brethren, watch!
  Be ye as men that wait
  All at the Master's gate,
  E'en though he tarry late,
   Watch, brethren, watch!

3 Heed we the Steward's call,
   Work, brethren, work!
  There's work enough for all:
   Work, brethren, work!
  This vineyard of the Lord
  Fresh labor will afford;
  Yours is a sure reward,
   Work, brethren, work!

4 Hear we the Shepherd's voice,
   Pray, brethren, pray!
  Would ye his heart rejoice?
   Pray, brethren, pray!
  Sin calls for constant fear,
  Long as we struggle here,
  We need the Strong One near,—
   Pray, brethren, pray!

5 Now sound the final chord,
   Praise, brethren, praise!
  Thrice holy is our Lord,
   Praise, brethren, praise!
  What more befits our tongues,
  Leading the angels' songs,
  While heaven the note prolongs?
   Praise, brethren, praise!

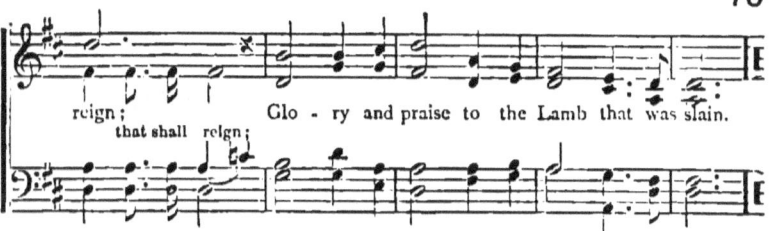

reign; glo-ry and praise to the Lamb that was slain.
that shall reign;

3 Can my lips be mute, or my heart be sad,
When the gracious Master hath made me glad?
When he points where the many mansions be,
And sweetly says, 'There is one for thee'?

4 I shall catch the gleam of its jasper wall
When I come to the gloom of the evenfall,
For I know that the shadows, dreary and dim,
Have a path of light that will lead to him.

From "Gems of Praise," by per.

My All to Thee.

HAVERGAL.   T. C. O'KANE. By per.

1. I bring my *sins* to thee, The sins I can-not count,
That all may cleansed be In thy once o-pen'd fount;
I bring them, Saviour, all to thee, The burden is too great for me: me.

2 My *heart* to thee I bring,
   The heart I cannot read;
   A faithless, wand'ring thing—
   An evil heart indeed;
I bring it, Saviour, now to thee,
That fixed and faithful it may be.

3 I bring my *grief* to thee,
   The grief I cannot tell,
   No words shall needed be,
   Thou knowest all so well;
I bring the sorrow laid on me,
O suffering Saviour, all to thee.

4 My *joys* to thee I bring,
   The joys thy love has given,
   That each may be a wing
   To lift me nearer heaven;
I bring them, Saviour, all to thee,
Who hast procured them all for me.

5 My *life* I bring to thee,
   I would not be my own;
   O Saviour, let me be
   Thine, ever thine alone:
My heart, my life, my all, I bring
To thee, my Saviour and my King.

76 More Like Thee.

"A."   Jno. R. Sweney.

1. Saviour, make me more like thee; This my constant prayer shall be: More like thee in heart and mind, More submissive, more resigned; More like thee in daily life, Free from anger, free from strife; That I may be more like thee, Savior, come, abide with me.

2. Saviour, make me more like thee; This my song, and this my plea: More like thee in word and deed, More like thee to those in need; Full of sympathy and love; Give me wisdom from above; That I may be more like thee, Draw me closer, Lord, to thee.

3. Saviour, I would ever be Daily growing more like thee: Lowly, gentle, patient, meek,—All thy graces, Lord, I seek: All thy mind to me impart; Wash my hands, my head, my heart! Thou did'st come to be like me, By and by I'll be like thee.

Chorus.

Saviour, make me more like thee, Saviour, make me more like thee, This my constant prayer shall be,—Saviour, make more like thee.

Copyright, 1873, by JOHN J. HOOD.

Christ Our Leader.

T. C. O'Kane. By per.

1. Children of the Heavenly King, As we journey let us sing;
Sing our Saviour's worthy praise, Glorious in his works and ways.
Glory, glory, hallelujah! Glory, glory, hallelujah!

REFRAIN.
Glory, glory, hallelujah! Christ our Leader bids us come;
Glory, glory, hallelujah! We are on our journey home.

2 We are trav'ling home to God,
In the way our fathers trod;
They are happy now, and we
Soon their happiness shall see.

3 O ye banished seed, be glad!
Christ our advocate is made;
Us to save our flesh assumes,
Brother to our souls becomes.

4 Fear not, brethren, joyful stand
On the borders of our land;
Jesus Christ, our Father's Son,
Bids us undismayed go on.

5 Lord, obediently we'll go,
Gladly leaving all below:
Only thou our leader be,
And we still will follow thee.

Remember Jesus Leads.

Words arranged.
Wm. J. Kirkpatrick

1. Ye sol-diers, to the charge go forth, Your Leader's call o-bey;
   Stay not till all the tribes of earth Shall own his sov'reign sway:
   Go, seek the souls that erring stray, For them a Sav-iour pleads, And while you keep the narrow way, Re-member Je-sus leads.

CHORUS.
Remember, remember, remember Je-sus leads;
Remember Jesus leads, re-member Jesus leads, Remember, oh, remember Jesus leads, Jesus leads;
Who trust in him are blest, He leads to per-fect rest; Oh, re-member Je-sus leads!
oh, re-member Je-sus leads, Je-sus leads!

2 His faithful ones, who ever strive
  His righteous cause to win,
Shall see their Master's work revive,
  His vict'ry over sin.
A fallen world in darkness lies,
  Each to the rescue speeds;
Though foes on every side arise,
  Remember Jesus leads.

3 Go up against sin's fortress walls,
  Go in the strength of grace;
And if a standard-bearer falls,
  Then you must take his place.
Oh, tell his love, that cannot fail,
  Make known his glorious deeds,
And tho' you walk thro' death's dark [vale,
  Remember Jesus leads.

From " Leaflet Gems, No. 1," by per.

Yield not to Temptation.

H. R. Palmer. By per.

1. Yield not to tempta-tion, For yielding is sin, Each victr'y will help you some oth-er to win; Fight manfully onward, Dark passions sub-due,
2. Shun e-vil companions, Bad language disdain, God's name hold in rev'rence, nor take it in vain; Be thoughtful and earnest, Kind-hearted and true,
3. To him that o'ercometh God giveth a crown, Thro' faith we will conquer, though often cast down; He who is our Saviour, Our strength will renew,

CHORUS.

Look ev-er to Je-sus, He'll car-ry you through. Ask the Saviour to help you, Comfort, strengthen, and keep you, He is willing to aid you, He will carry you through.

STAND UP FOR JESUS.—Webb, key B flat.

1 Stand up! stand up for Jesus!
  Ye soldiers of the cross;
  Lift high his royal banner,
  It must not suffer loss;
  From victory unto victory
  His army he shall lead,
  Till every foe is vanquished,
  And Christ is Lord indeed.

2 Stand up! stand up for Jesus!
  Stand in his strength alone;
  The arm of flesh will fail you,—
  Ye dare not trust your own;
  Put on the gospel armor,
  And, watching unto prayer,
  Where duty calls, or danger,
  Be never wanting there.

3 Stand up! stand up for Jesus!
  The strife will not be long;
  This day the noise of battle,
  The next the victor's song;
  To him that overcometh
  A crown of life shall be,
  He with the King of Glory
  Shall reign eternally.

The Great Physician.

2 Your many sins are all forgiven,
  Oh, hear the voice of Jesus;
  Go on your way in peace to heaven,
  And wear a crown with Jesus.
3 All glory to the dying Lamb!
  I now believe in Jesus;
  I love the blessed Saviour's name,
  I love the name of Jesus.
4 The children too, both great and small,
  Who love the name of Jesus,
  May now accept his gracious call
  To work and live for Jesus.

5 Come, brethren, help me sing his praise,
  Oh, praise the name of Jesus;
  Come, sisters, all your voices raise,
  Oh, bless the name of Jesus.
6 His name dispels my guilt and fear,
  No other name but Jesus;
  Oh, how my soul delights to hear
  The precious name of Jesus.
7 And when to that bright world above,
  We rise to see our Jesus,
  We'll sing around the throne of love
  His name, the name of Jesus.

MY SOUL, BE ON THY GUARD.—Laban, key D.

1 My soul, be on thy guard,
  Ten thousand foes arise;
  The hosts of sin are pressing hard
  To draw thee from the skies.
2 Oh, watch, and fight, and pray;
  The battle ne'er give o'er;
  Renew it boldly every day,
  And help divine implore.

3 Ne'er think the vict'ry won,
  Nor lay thine armor down;
  The work of faith will not be done
  Till thou obtain the crown.
4 Then persevere till death
  Shall bring thee to thy God;
  He'll take thee, at thy parting breath,
  To his divine abode.

Faithful Guide. 81

M. M. WELLS. By per.

1. Ho-ly Spir-it, faith-ful guide, Ev-er near the Christian's side;
Gen-tly lead us by the hand, Pil-grims in a des-ert land;
D.C. Whisp'ring soft-ly, wan d'rer, come! Follow me, I'll guide thee home.

Wea-ry souls for e'er re-joice, While they hear that sweet-est voice,

2 Ever present, truest Friend,
Ever near thine aid to lend,
Leave us not to doubt and fear,
Groping on in darkness drear,
When the storms are raging sore,
Hearts grow faint, and hopes give o'er,
Whispering softly, wanderer, come!
Follow me, I'll guide thee home.

3 When our days of toil shall cease,
Waiting still for sweet release,
Nothing left but heaven and prayer,
Wond'ring if our names were there;
Wading deep the dismal flood,
Pleading nought but Jesus' blood;
Whispering softly, wanderer, come!
Follow me, I'll guide thee home!

Call to Praise.—Laban. S. M.

1. Stand up, and bless the Lord, Ye peo-ple of his choice;
Stand up and bless the Lord your God With heart, and soul, and voice.

2 Though high above all praise,
  Above all blessing high,
Who would not fear his holy name,
  And laud and magnify?

3 Oh, for the living flame,
  From his own altar brought,
To touch our lips, our souls inspire,
  And wing to heaven our thought!

4 God is our strength and song,
  And his salvation ours;
Then be his love in Christ proclaimed
  With all our ransomed powers.

5 Stand up, and bless the Lord,
  The Lord your God adore;
Stand up, and bless his glorious name,
  Henceforth, forevermore!

F

82. Do We Always Tell the Story?

Selected.   J. H. KURZENKNABE.   Chorus, *Nettleton.*

1. Do we al-ways tell the sto-ry Of the Saviour's wondrous love?
2. Tell the sto-ry to the faint-ing, As they ling-er on the road;
3. I have oft-en heard the sto-ry, Yet, 'tis sweet-er far to me
4. Tell me, last of all, the sto-ry, When the light of life grows dim;

Do we al-ways seek his glo-ry, And his boundless mer-cy prove?
Tell them of the bles-sed Saviour, How he helps to bear the load:
Than it was when first I heard it, Prom-is-ing sal-va-tion free:
Of the Saviour and his glo-ry, Tell me, last of all, of him:

Let us kind-ly tell our neighbor Of the thorns that pierced his brow,
Tell them of a home e-ter-nal, Of the mansions waiting now,
When my soul is sore-ly tempted, When dark shadows cloud my brow,
Would you kindly soothe the aching Of my fevered, throbbing brow,

Of the life he gave to save them, Tell them when, and where, and how.
Tell that Je-sus has pre-pared them, Tell them when, and where, and how.
Come and tell me that he suf-fer'd, Tell me when, and where, and how.
Tell me that he died to save me, Tell me when, and where, and how.

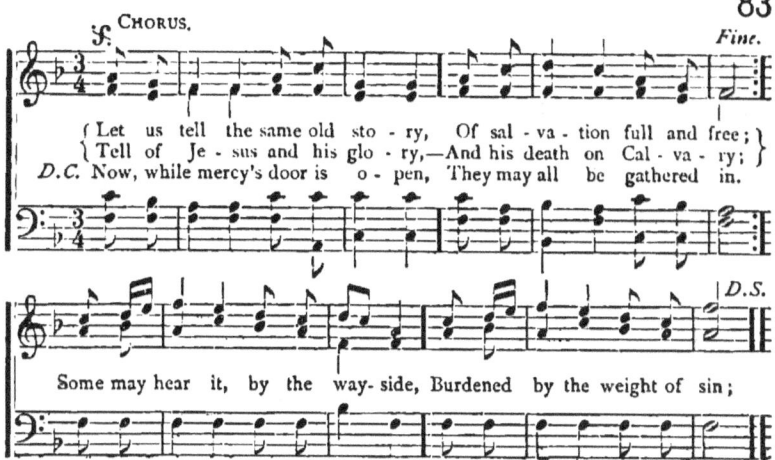

CHORUS.
Fine.
Let us tell the same old sto - ry, Of sal - va - tion full and free;
Tell of Je - sus and his glo - ry,—And his death on Cal - va - ry;
D.C. Now, while mercy's door is o - pen, They may all be gathered in.
D.S.
Some may hear it, by the way- side, Burdened by the weight of sin;

From "Song Treasury," by per.

Loving Jesus.

H. L. B. [INFANT CLASS.] HARRY L. BROOKS.

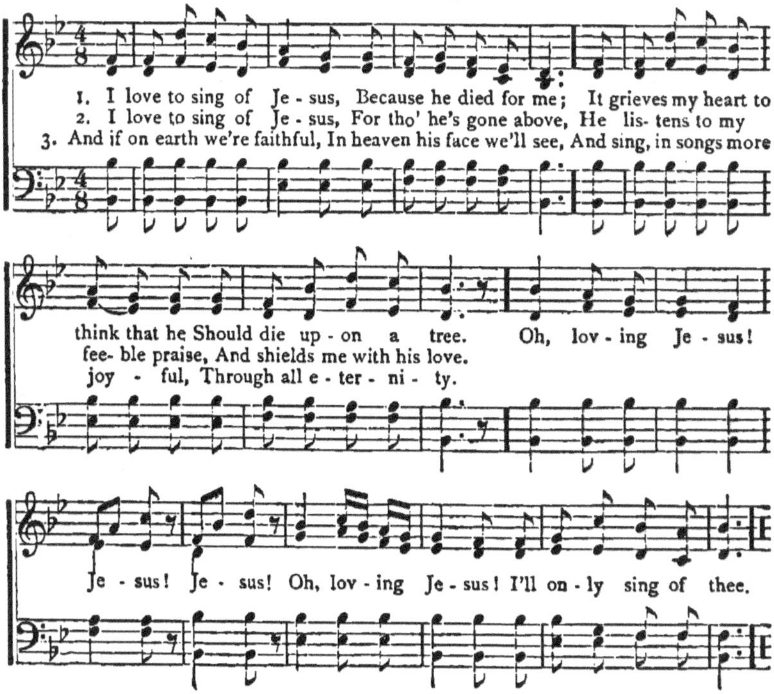
1. I love to sing of Je - sus, Because he died for me; It grieves my heart to think that he Should die up - on a tree.
2. I love to sing of Je - sus, For tho' he's gone above, He lis- tens to my fee- ble praise, And shields me with his love.
3. And if on earth we're faithful, In heaven his face we'll see, And sing, in songs more joy - ful, Through all e - ter - ni - ty.
Oh, lov - ing Je - sus! Je - sus! Je - sus! Oh, lov - ing Je - sus! I'll on - ly sing of thee.

Rev. J. H. Stockton.

2 I love my precious Saviour,
  Because he died for me,
And if I did not serve him,
  How sinful I would be;
He gives me every comfort,
  And hears me when I pray;
I want to live for Jesus,
  The Bible says I may.

3 I now can do a little,
  But when I am a man
I'll try to do for Jesus
  The greatest good I can;
God help and keep me faithful
  In all I do and say,
I want to live a Christian,
  The Bible says I may.

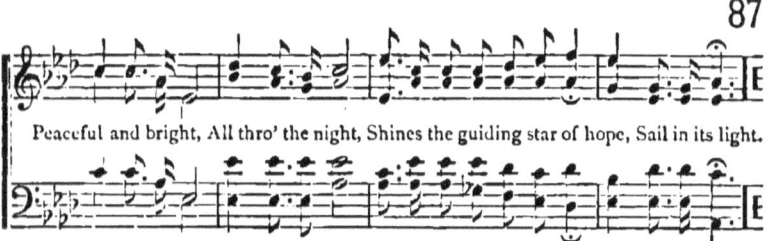

Peaceful and bright, All thro' the night, Shines the guiding star of hope, Sail in its light.

The New Name.

J. E. H.   J. E. Hall.

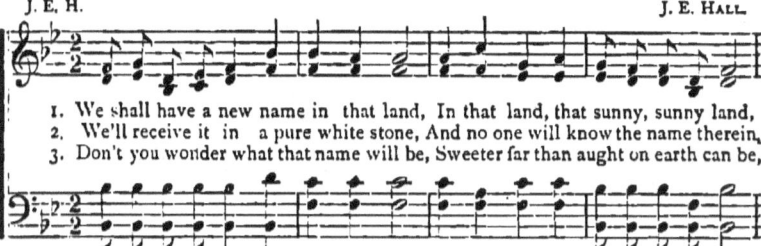

1. We shall have a new name in that land, In that land, that sunny, sunny land,
2. We'll receive it in a pure white stone, And no one will know the name therein,
3. Don't you wonder what that name will be, Sweeter far than aught on earth can be,

Cho.— *We shall have a new name in that land, In that land, that sunny, sunny land,*

When we meet that bright angelic band, In that sunny land. A new name, a new name
Only unto him who hath 'tis known, When we're free from sin. A white stone, a white stone
We will be quite satisfied when we Shall that new name know. I wonder, I won-der

When we meet that bright angelic band, In that sunny land.

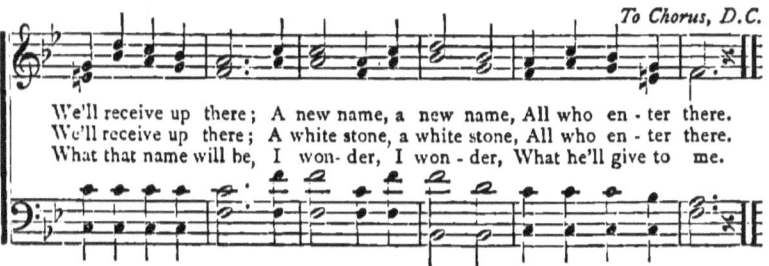

We'll receive up there; A new name, a new name, All who en-ter there.
We'll receive up there; A white stone, a white stone, All who en-ter there.
What that name will be, I won-der, I won-der, What he'll give to me.

Grateful Praise

PRELUDE (*to each verse*).   W. B. EVANS.

Let us praise the Lord, Oh, praise his name, Let us bless his ho-ly name.

1. { We bring no glit-t'ring trea-sures, No gems from earth's deep mine;
{ Children, thy fa-vor shar-ing, Their voice of thanks would raise;

We come with sim-ple mea-sures To chant thy love di-vine.
Fa-ther, ac-cept our of-f'ring, Our song of grate-ful praise.

CHORUS.

We praise thee, Lord, We mag-ni-fy thy name, We
We praise, we bless, We mag-ni-fy and bless thy name,

praise thee, Lord, We bless and mag-ni-fy thy name.
We praise, we bless,

Let us praise the Lord, etc.

2 The dearest gift of Heaven,
   Love's written Word of Truth,
To us is early given,
   To guide our steps in youth;
We hear the wondrous story,
   The tale of Calvary;
We read of homes in glory,
   From sin and sorrow free.

Let us praise the Lord, etc.

3 Redeemer, grant thy blessing;
   Oh, teach us how to pray,
That each, thy fear possessing,
   May tread life's onward way;
Then where the pure are dwelling
   We hope to meet again,
And sweeter anthems swelling,
   Forever praise thy name.

Let Us Seek Salvation To-day.

JOSEPHINE POLLARD. FRANK M. DAVIS.

1. We nev-er shall be hap-py if we walk the way of sin, 'Tis a
2. We'll nev-er get to heav-en if we do not learn the way, And pre-
3. The Tempter may as-sail us, but with Je-sus by our side, And a

path that leads onward to sorrow; If the right we would pur-sue, it is
pare for the journey be-fore us; If for Je-sus we would live, we must
hope in his pow-er possessing; We will make his ho-ly word still our

time we should be-gin; For why need we wait for to-mor-row?
always watch and pray, And thus will his ban-ner be o'er us.
counsel and our guide, And count ev-'ry tri-al a blessing.

CHORUS.

Let us seek salva-tion to-day, Let us seek salva-tion to-day, If the
yes, to-day, yes, to-day,

crown we would secure, We must make our calling sure, And seek salvation to-day.

From "New Pearls of Song," by permission.

94. Come to the Royal Fountain.

WM. H. CLARK.　　　　　　　　　　WM. J. KIRKPATRICK.

1. See where the liv-ing waters glide, From David's house they sweetly flow;
Who wash-es in the cleansing tide Is whit-er than the driven snow.

CHORUS.
Then, come to the roy-al foun-tain! Ev-er in its stream a-bide;
Come to the roy-al foun-tain, O-pen'd in the Sav-iour's side.

2 It flows, an ever-running stream,—
 Free as the fountain of his grace
Who died, that he might thus redeem
 The fallen sons of Adam's race.

3 Down through the ages flowing wide,—
 Its virtue is to-day the same
As when from out his pierced side
 The mingled tide of blessing came.

4 Whoever will, may drink and live;
 New life the healing draught inspires.
From those who nothing have to give,
 The royal bounty naught requires.

5 All over Canaan's goodly land,
 Where saints enjoy a sweet repose,
'Mid pastures green, on every hand
 King David's royal fountain flows.

From " Leaflet Gems, No. 1," by per.

The Rifted Rock.

1. In the Rift-ed Rock I'm resting, Safe-ly shelter'd I a-bide,
There no foes nor storms mo-lest me, While within the cleft I hide.

2. Long pur-sued by sin and Sa-tan, Wea-ry, sad, I long'd for rest,
Then I found this heavenly shelter, O-pen'd in my Sa-viour's breast.

CHORUS.
Now I'm resting, sweet-ly rest-ing, In the cleft once made for me;
Je-sus, bles-sed Rock of A-ges, I will hide my-self in thee.

3 Peace which passeth understanding,
Joy the world can never give
Now in Jesus I am finding,
In his smiles of love I live.
Now I'm resting, etc.

4 In the Rifted Rock I'll hide me
Till the storms of life are past,
All secure in this blest refuge,
Heeding not the fiercest blast.
Now I'm resting, etc.

AM I A SOLDIER OF THE CROSS. C. M.

1 Am I a soldier of the cross,—
 A foll'wer of the Lamb,—
 And shall I fear to own his cause,
 Or blush to speak his name?

2 Must I be carried to the skies
 On flowery beds of ease;
 While others fought to win the prize,
 And sailed through bloody seas?

3 Are there no foes for me to face?
 Must I not stem the flood?
 Is this vile world a friend to grace,
 To help me on to God?

4 Since I must fight if I would reign,
 Increase my courage, Lord;
 I'll bear the toil, endure the pain,
 Supported by thy Word.

Going Home.

Rev E A Hoffman — Jno. J. Hood.

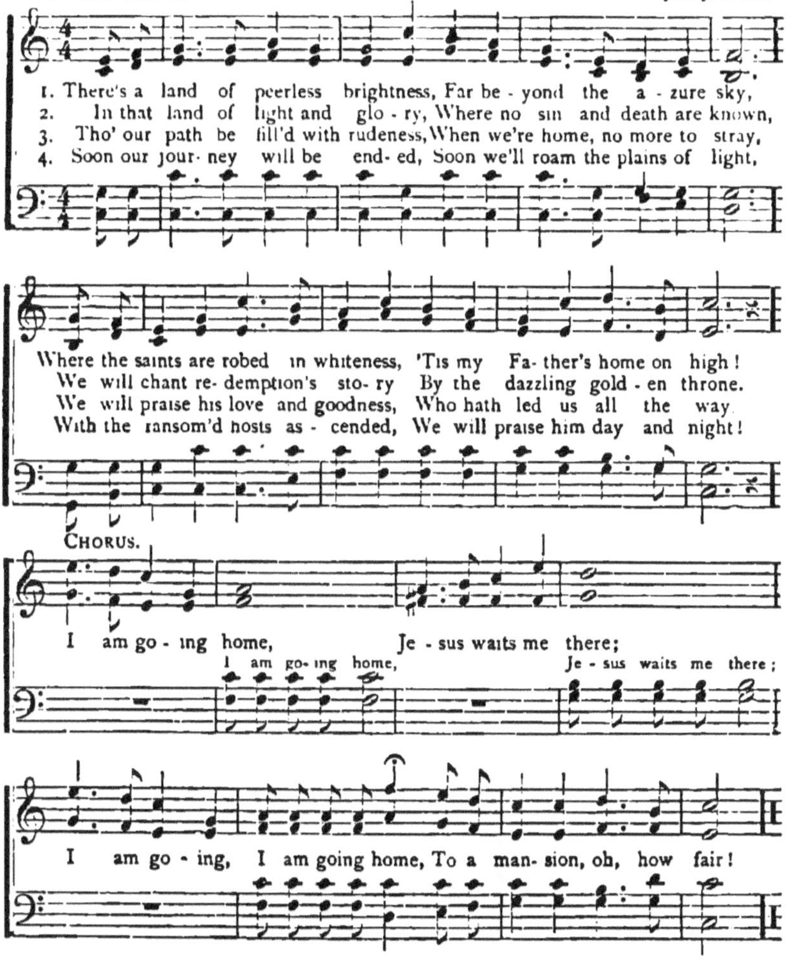
1. There's a land of peerless brightness, Far be - yond the a - zure sky,
2. In that land of light and glo - ry, Where no sin and death are known,
3. Tho' our path be fill'd with rudeness, When we're home, no more to stray,
4. Soon our jour- ney will be end- ed, Soon we'll roam the plains of light,
Where the saints are robed in whiteness, 'Tis my Fa- ther's home on high!
We will chant re- demption's sto- ry By the dazzling gold - en throne.
We will praise his love and goodness, Who hath led us all the way.
With the ransom'd hosts as - cended, We will praise him day and night!
Chorus.
I am go - ing home, Je - sus waits me there;
I am go- ing home, Je - sus waits me there;
I am go - ing, I am going home, To a man- sion, oh, how fair!

HE LEADETH ME.—Key D.

1 He leadeth me! oh, blessed thought!
Oh, words with heavenly comfort fraught!
Whate'er I do, where'er I be,
Still 'tis God's hand that leadeth me.

REFRAIN.

He leadeth me! he leadeth me!
By his own hand he leadeth me;
His faithful follower I would be,
For by his hand he leadeth me.

2 Sometimes mid scenes of deepest gloom,
Sometimes where Eden's bowers bloom,
By waters still, o'er troubled sea,—
Still 'tis his hand that leadeth me.

3 Lord, I would clasp thy hand in mine,
Nor ever murmur nor repine,—
Content, whatever lot I see,
Since 'tis my God that leadeth me.

4 And when my task on earth is done,
When by thy grace the victory's won,
E'en death's cold wave I will not flee,
Since God through Jordan leadeth me.

The Syren's Song.

FLORA B. HARRIS.
JNO. R. SWENEY.

1. See! the pur-ple wine is flow-ing, See! its ro-sy lights are glow-ing,
2. Many a crystal fount is streaming, In the golden sun-light gleaming;
3. God's free heaven smiles a-bove thee, While its angels stoop to love thee,

While, with dread and subtle beau-ty, Luring men from truth and du-ty,
Chiming with its fai-ry voic-es, Till the thirsting earth re-joic-es,—
With up-lift-ed hand and vis-ion, Pointing to their home e-lys-ian;

Soft a sy-ren's voice is call-ing, On the air in mu-sic fall-ing:
"Come and quaff my sparkling treas-ure, Bubbling forth in boundless meas-ure;
Sin and death re-peat their sto-ry, In the wine-cup's crimson glo-ry:

'Tis the old-en, fa-tal cry, "Drink, O mor-tal, drink, and die!"
Tho' as sweet as ev-'ning's sigh Sings the sy-ren, drink, and die!"
Like a star, se-rene and high, Set thy pur-pose in the sky!

CHORUS.

Oh, for God and right be strong, Turning from the syren's song;
for right be strong, the syren's song.

Copyright, 1878, by JOHN J. HOOD.

Who hath Sorrow?

"Who hath woe? who hath sorrow? who hath contentions? who hath babbling? who hath wounds without cause? who hath redness of eyes? They that tarry long at the wine." —Pr. 23, 29.

JNO. R. SWENEY.

1. Who hath sor-row? who hath woe? Who hath babbling? who hath strife?
2. They that tar-ry at the wine, They that love the feast and song;
3. Drinker, turn, and leave the bowl,—Drunkards can not en-ter heav'n;

Who to swift de-struc-tion go, Turn-ing from the path of life?
They that fier-y drinks combine, Ear-ly haste, and tar-ry long.
Christ hath died to save thy soul, Flee to him, and be forgiven.

CHORUS.
Who hath sor-row? who hath woe? They that tar-ry long at the wine;
Who hath sor-row? who hath woe? They that tar-ry long at the wine.

BROTHERS! RALLY FOR THE CONFLICT.—*Tune, HOLD THE FORT.*

1 Brothers! rally for the conflict,
  See the banner wave;
  Temperance bands are pressing onward,
  Fallen men to save.
  *Hear a mighty host of freemen
  Songs of triumph raise;
  Love hath conquered, chains are broken;
  Give to God the praise.*

2 Swift the day of life is passing,
  Soon will fall the night;
  Urge we then the glorious conflict,
  Battling for the right.

3 Led no more by passion captive,
  Haunts of vice we shun;
  Happy hearts and smiling faces
  Tell of victory won.

WM. STEVENSON.

CHORUS.

breaks my heart to think that I Am called a drunkard's child. But,
father dear, 'tis sad to see That drink has changed you so. And,
oh, how much I wish that God Would on-ly let me die! For,
from a life of want and woe, You'll save your weeping child. For,

oh! my heart is ve-ry sad, My brain is al-most wild; It

breaks my heart to think that I Am called a drunkard's child.

Sign the Pledge.

J. H. J.   Slave Melody.

1. :||: Come and sign the pledge to-night, boys, :||: Be slaves to drink no more.
2. :||: God will give you strength to keep it, :||: If you his grace implore.

SAY, BROTHER.

1 :||: Say, brother, will you meet us :||: On Canaan's happy shore?
2 :||: Say, sister, will you meet us :||: On Canaan's happy shore?
3 :||: That will be a happy meeting :||: On Canaan's happy shore!
4 :||: Jesus lives and reigns forever :||: On Canaan's happy shore!
5 :||: Glory! glory! hallelujah! :||: Forever, evermore!

Come, Thou Fount.

Tune, NETTLETON.

1 Come, thou fount of every blessing,
   Tune my heart to sing thy grace;
Streams of mercy, never ceasing,
   Call for songs of loudest praise.
Teach me some melodious sonnet,
   Sung by flaming tongues above;
Praise the mount! I'm fixed upon it,
   Mount of God's unchanging love!

2 Here I'll raise my Ebenezer;
   Hither by thy help I'm come;
And I hope, by thy good pleasure,
   Safely to arrive at home.

Jesus sought me when a stranger,
   Wandering from the fold of God;
He, to rescue me from danger,
   Interposed his precious blood.

3 Oh, to grace how great a debtor
   Daily I'm constrained to be!
Let thy goodness, like a fetter,
   Bind my wand'ring heart to thee.
Prone to wander, Lord, I feel it,
   Prone to leave the God I love,—
Here's my heart; oh, take and seal it,
   Seal it for thy courts above.

WELCOME, WELCOME, DEAR REDEEMER.—*Tune,* NETTLETON.

1 Welcome, welcome, dear Redeemer,
   Welcome to this heart of mine;
Lord, I make a full surrender,
   Every power and thought be thine;}
     Thine entirely,
Through eternal ages thine.

2 Known to all to be thy mansion,
   Earth and hell will disappear;
Or in vain attempt possession,
   When they find the Lord is near;
     Shout, O Zion!
Shout, ye saints! the Lord is here.

Vespers. 8s, & 7s.

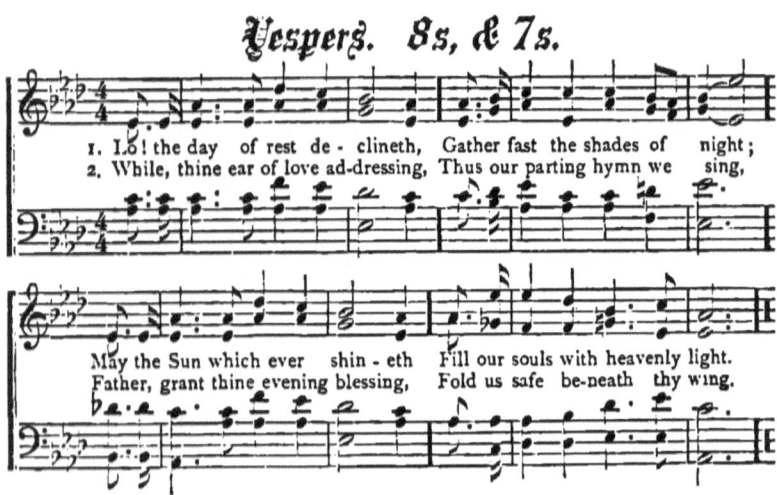

1. Lo! the day of rest declineth, Gather fast the shades of night;
   May the Sun which ever shineth Fill our souls with heavenly light.
2. While, thine ear of love addressing, Thus our parting hymn we sing,
   Father, grant thine evening blessing, Fold us safe beneath thy wing.

Retreat. L. M. 109

1 From every stormy wind that blows,
From every swelling tide of woes,
There is a calm, a sure retreat;
'Tis found beneath the mercy-seat.

2 There is a place where Jesus sheds
The oil of gladness on our heads,—
A place than all besides more sweet;
It is the blood-bought mercy-seat.

3 There is a scene where spirits blend,
Where friend holds fellowship with friend;
Though sundered far, by faith they meet
Around one common mercy-seat.

4 There, there on eagle wings we soar,
And time and sense seem all no more,
And heav'n comes down our souls to greet,
And glory crowns the mercy-seat.

Cross and Crown.

1 Must Jesus bear the cross alone,
And all the world go free?
No; there's a cross for every one,
And there's a cross for me.

2 The consecrated cross I'll bear,
Till death shall set me free,
And then go home my crown to wear,
For there's a crown for me.

3 Upon the crystal pavement, down
At Jesus pierc-ed feet,
Joyful I'll cast my golden crown,
And his dear name repeat.

4 Oh, precious cross! oh, glorious crown!
Oh, resurrection day!
Ye angels, from the stars come down,
And bear my soul away.

LORD, DISMISS US.—*Sicily.*

1 Lord, dismiss us with thy blessing;
  Fill our hearts with joy and peace;
  Let us each, thy love possessing,
  Triumph in redeeming grace;
    O refresh us,
  Travelling through this wilderness.

2 Thanks we give, and adoration,
  For thy gospel's joyful sound;
  May the fruits of thy salvation
  In our hearts and lives abound;
    May thy presence
  With us evermore be found.

3 So, whene'er the signal's given
  Us from earth to call away,
  Borne on angels' wings to heaven,
  Glad the summons to obey,
    May we ever
  Reign with Christ in endless day.

BLEST BE THE TIE.—*Dennis.*

1 Blest be the tie that binds
    Our hearts in Christian love;
  The fellowship of kindred minds
    Is like to that above.

2 Before our Father's throne
    We pour our ardent prayers;
  Our fears, our hopes, our aims are one,—
    Our comforts and our cares.

3 We share our mutual woes;
    Our mutual burdens bear;
  And often for each other flows
    The sympathizing tear.

4 When we assunder part,
    It gives us inward pain;
  But we shall still be joined in heart,
    And hope to meet again.

Antioch. C. M.

O FOR A THOUSAND TONGUES.—Antioch.

1 O for a thousand tongues, to sing
   My great Redeemer's praise;
   The glories of my God and King,
   The triumphs of his grace.

   My gracious Master, and my God,
   Assist me to proclaim,—
   To spread, through all the earth abroad,
   The honors of thy name.

3 Jesus! the name that charms our fears,
   That bids our sorrows cease;
   'Tis music in the sinner's ears,
   'Tis life, and health, and peace.

4 He breaks the power of cancell'd sin,
   He sets the pris'ner free;
   His blood can make the foulest clean;
   His blood availed for me.

HARK, THE GLAD SOUND.—Antioch.

1 Hark, the glad sound! the Saviour comes,
   The Saviour, promised long;
   Let every heart prepare a throne,
   And every voice a song.

2 He comes, the pris'ner to release,
   In Satan's bondage held;
   The gates of brass before him burst,
   The iron fetters yield.

3 He comes, from thickest films of vice
   To clear the mental ray,
   And on the eyes oppressed with night
   To pour celestial day.

4 Our glad hosannas, Prince of Peace,
   Thy welcome shall proclaim,
   And heaven's eternal arches ring
   With thy beloved name.

JOY TO THE WORLD.—Antioch.

1 Joy to the world, the Lord is come!
   Let earth receive her King;
   Let every heart prepare him room,
   And heaven and nature sing.

2 Joy to the world, the Saviour reigns!
   Let men their songs employ;
   While fields and floods, rocks, hills, and
   Repeat the sounding joy.   [plains,

3 No more let sin and sorrow grow,
   Nor thorns infest the ground;
   He comes to make his blessings flow
   Far as the curse is found.

4 He rules the world with truth and grace,
   And makes the nations prove
   The glories of his righteousness,
   And wonders of his love.

DOXOLOGY. C. M.

To Father, Son, and Holy Ghost,
One God, whom we adore,
Be glory as it was, is now,
And shall be evermore.

1   SICILY.—E.

1 Guide me, O thou great Jehovah,
   Pilgrim thro' this barren land;
   I am weak, but thou art mighty,
   Hold me with thy powerful hand;
   Bread of heaven,
   Feed me till I want no more.

2 Open now the crystal fountain,
   Whence the healing waters flow;
   Let the fiery, cloudy pillar
   Lead me all my journey through;
   Strong Deliverer,
   Be thou still my strength and shield.

3 When I tread the verge of Jordan,
   Bid my anxious fears subside;
   Bear me thro' the swelling current,
   Land me safe on Canaan's side;
   Songs of praises
   I will ever give to thee.

2   —o—   KEY D.

1 Sweet hour of prayer! sweet hour of prayer!
   That calls me from a world of care,
   And bids me at my Father's throne
   Make all my wants and wishes known:
   In seasons of distress and grief
   My soul has often found relief,
:|: And oft' escaped the tempter's snare
   By thy return, sweet hour of prayer. :||:

2 Sweet hour of prayer! sweet hour of prayer!
   Thy wings shall my petition bear
   To him whose truth and faithfulness
   Engage the waiting soul to bless:
   And since he bids me seek his face,
   Believe his word, and trust his grace,
:||: I'll cast on him my every care,
   And wait for thee, sweet hour of prayer.|:

3   FOUNTAIN.—C.

1 There is a fountain filled with blood
   Drawn from Immanuel's veins,
   And sinners plunged beneath that flood
   Lose all their guilty stains.

2 The dying thief rejoiced to see
   That fountain in his day;
   And there may I, though vile as he,
   Wash all my sins away.

3 E'er since by faith I saw the stream
   Thy flowing wounds supply,
   Redeeming love has been my theme,
   And shall be till I die.

4 Then in a nobler, sweeter song
   I'll sing thy power to save, [tongue
   When this poor, lisping, stammering
   Lies silent in the grave.

4   KEY F.

1 What a Friend we have in Jesus,
   All our sins and griefs to bear!
   What a privilege to carry
   Everything to God in prayer.
   Oh, what peace we often forfeit,
   Oh, what needless pain we bear,
   All because we do not carry
   Everything to God in prayer.

2 Have we trials and temptations?
   Is there trouble anywhere?
   We should never be discouraged,
   Take it to the Lord in prayer.
   Can we find a Friend so faithful,
   Who will all our sorrows share?
   Jesus knows our every weakness,
   Take it to the Lord in prayer.

3 Are we weak and heavy laden,
   Cumbered with a load of care?
   Precious Saviour, still our Refuge,—
   Take it to the Lord in prayer.
   Do thy friends despise, forsake thee?
   Take it to the Lord in prayer;
   In his arms he'll take and shield thee,
   Thou wilt find a solace there.

5   —o—   KEY C.

1 There is a gate that stands ajar,
   And through its portals gleaming,
   A radiance from the cross, afar
   The Saviour's love revealing.

CHO.—*Oh, depth of mercy, can it be,*
   That gate was left ajar for me!
   For me, for me,
   Was left ajar for me!

2 That gate ajar stands free for all
   Who seek through it salvation,—
   The rich and poor, the great and small
   Of every tribe and nation.

3 Press onward, then, tho' foes may frown,
   While mercy's gate is open;
   Accept the cross, and win the crown,
   Love's everlasting token.

6   NAOMI.—D.

1 Father, whate'er of earthly bliss
   Thy sov'reign will denies,
   Accepted at thy throne of grace,
   Let this petition rise;

2 "Give me a calm, a thankful heart,
   From every murmur free;
   The blessings of thy grace impart,
   And make me live to thee.

3 Let the sweet hope that thou art mine
   My life and death attend;
   Thy presence through my journey shine,
   And crown my journey's end."

7   KEY A.

1. Oh, think of the home over there,
   By the side of the river of life,
   Where the saints, all immortal and fair,
   Are robed in their garments of white.
   REFRAIN.
   Over there, over there,
   Oh, think of a home over there!

2. Oh, think of the friends over there,
   Who before us the journey have trod,
   Of the songs that they breathe on the air
   In their home in the palace of God.

3. My Saviour is now over there, [rest,
   There my kindred and friends are at
   Then, away from my sorrow and care,
   Let me fly to the land of the blest.

8   —o—   KEY C.

1. Sowing the seed by the daylight fair,
   Sowing the seed by the noon-day glare,
   Sowing the seed by the fading light,
   Sowing the seed in the solemn night;
   Oh, what shall the harvest be?
   CHORUS.
   Sown in the darkness or sown in the light,
   Sown in our weakness or sown in our
   Gathered in time or eternity, [*might,*
   Sure, ah, sure will the harvest be.

2. Sowing the seed by the wayside high,
   Sowing the seed on the rocks to die,
   Sowing the seed where the thorns will spoil,
   Sowing the seed in the fertile soil;
   Oh, what shall the harvest be?

3. Sowing the seed of a lingering pain,
   Sowing the seed of a maddened brain,
   Sowing the seed of a tarnished name,
   Sowing the seed of eternal shame;
   Oh, what shall the harvest be?

4. Sowing the seed with an aching heart,
   Sowing the seed while the teardrops start,
   Sowing in hope, till the reapers come,
   Gladly to gather the harvest home:
   Oh, what shall the harvest be?

9   —o—   KEY F.

1. To-day the Saviour calls,
   Ye wand'rers, come;
   O ye benighted souls,
   Why longer roam?

2. To-day the Saviour calls;
   O listen now;
   Within these sacred walls
   To Jesus bow.

3. The Spirit calls to-day:
   Yield to his power;
   Oh, grieve him not away
   'Tis mercy's hour.

H

10   KEY G.

1. I have a Saviour, he's pleading in glory,
   A dear, loving Saviour, tho' earth-friends be few;
   And now he is watching in tenderness o'er me,
   And oh that my Saviour were your Saviour too.
   CHO.—:|: *For you I am praying,:|:*
   I'm praying for you.

2. I have a Father, to me he has given
   A hope for eternity, blessed and true:
   And soon will he call me to meet him in heaven, [me too.
   But oh that he'd let me bring you with

3. I have a peace; it is calm as a river,—
   A peace that the friends of this world never knew,
   My Saviour alone is its Author and Giver,
   And oh, could I know it was given to you!

11   —o—   OLIVET.—E♭

1. My faith looks up to thee,
   Thou Lamb of Calvary,
   Saviour divine;
   Now hear me while I pray;
   Take all my guilt away;
   O, let me from this day
   Be wholly thine.

2. May thy rich grace impart
   Strength to my fainting heart;
   My zeal inspire;
   As thou hast died for me,
   O may my love to thee
   Pure, warm, and changeless be,—
   A living fire.

3. While life's dark maze I tread,
   And griefs around me spread,
   Be thou my guide;
   Bid darkness turn to day;
   Wipe sorrow's tears away,
   Nor let me ever stray
   From thee aside.

12   —o—   CORONATION.—C.

1. All hail the power of Jesus' name!
   Let angels prostrate fall;
   Bring forth the royal diadem,
   And crown him Lord of all.

2. Let every kindred, every tribe,
   On this terrestrial ball,
   To him all majesty ascribe,
   And crown him Lord of all..

3. Oh that with yonder sacred throng
   We at his feet may fall;
   We'll join the everlasting song,
   And crown him Lord of all.

FAMILIAR HYMNS

13   LOVING-KINDNESS.—G.

1. Awake, my soul, in joyful lays,
And sing thy great Redeemer's praise,
He justly claims a song from thee,
His loving-kindness oh, how free!

2. He saw me ruined in the fall,
Yet loved me notwithstanding all;
He saved me from my lost estate,
His loving-kindness, oh, how great!

3. Often I feel my sinful heart
Prone from my Saviour to depart;
But, though I oft have him forgot,
His loving-kindness changes not.

4. Soon shall I pass the gloomy vale,
Soon all my mortal powers must fail;
Oh, may my last expiring breath
His loving-kindness sing in death.

14   —o—   KEY A♭

1. Oh, sometimes the shadows are deep,
And rough seems the path to the goal,
And sorrows, how often they sweep
Like tempests, down over the soul,
Oh, then, to the Rock let me fly!
To the Rock that is higher than I.

2. Oh, sometimes how long seems the day,
And sometimes how weary my feet;
But, toiling in life's dusty way,
The Rock's blessed shadow, how sweet!

3. Oh, near to the Rock let me keep,
Or blessings, or sorrows prevail;
Or climbing the mountain-way steep,
Or walking the shadowy vale.
                    E. JOHNSON.

15   —o—   KEY E♭

1. I hear thy welcome voice,
That calls me, Lord, to thee,
For cleansing in thy precious blood,
That flowed on Calvary.
I am coming, Lord,
Coming now to thee!
Wash me, cleanse me in the blood
That flowed on Calvary.

2. Though coming weak and vile,
Thou dost my strength assure;
Thou dost my vileness fully cleanse,
Till spotless all and pure.

3. 'Tis Jesus calls me on
To perfect faith and love,
To perfect hope, and peace, and trust,
For earth and heaven above.

4. All hail, atoning blood!
All hail, redeeming grace!
All hail, the gift of Christ our Lord,
Our Strength and Righteousness!
                    Rev. L. HARTSOUGH.

16   KEY F.

1. Knocking, knocking, who is there?
Waiting, waiting, oh, how fair!
'Tis a Pilgrim strange and kingly,
Never such was seen before:
Ah! my soul, for such a wonder,
Wilt thou not undo the door?

2. Knocking, knocking, still he's there,
Waiting, waiting, wondrous fair!
But the door is hard to open,
For the weeds and ivy vine,
With their dark and clinging tendrils,
Ever round the hinges twine.

3. Knocking, knocking—what, still there?
Waiting, waiting, grand and fair!
Yes, the pierced hand still knocketh,
And beneath the crowned hair
Beam the patient eyes, so tender,
Of thy Saviour, waiting there.
                    Mrs. H. B. STOWE.

17   TOPLADY.—B♭

1. Rock of Ages, cleft for me,
Let me hide myself in thee;
Let the water and the blood,
From thy wounded side which flowed,
Be of sin the double cure,—
Save from wrath, and make me pure.

2. Could my tears forever flow,
Could my zeal no languor know,
These for sin could not atone;
Thou must save, and thou alone;
In my hand no price I bring,
Simply to thy cross I cling.

3. While I draw this fleeting breath,
When my eyes shall close in death,
When I rise to worlds unknown,
And behold thee on thy throne,—
Rock of Ages, cleft for me,
Let me hide myself in thee.
                    TOPLADY.

18   SOLID ROCK—A.

1. My hope is built on nothing less
Than Jesus' blood and righteousness;
I dare not trust the sweetest frame,
But wholly lean on Jesus' name.
On Christ, the solid rock, I stand;
All other ground is sinking sand.

2. When darkness seems to veil his face,
I rest on his unchanging grace;
In every high and stormy gale,
My anchor holds within the veil.

3. His word, his covenant, and blood
Support me in the 'whelming flood;
When all around on earth gives way,
He then is all my help and stay.

19   KEY F.

1 Work, for the night is coming;
   Work through the morning hours;
   Work, while the dew is sparkling;
   Work, 'mid springing flowers;
   Work, when the day grows brighter;
   Work, in the glowing sun;
   Work, for the night is coming,
   When man's work is done.

2 Work, for the night is coming;
   Work through the sunny noon;
   Fill brightest hours with labor;
   Rest comes sure and soon.
   Give every flying minute
   Something to keep in store;
   Work, for the night is coming,
   When man works no more.

20   BETHANY.—G.

1 Nearer, my God, to thee,
    Nearer to thee!
   E'en though it be a cross
    That raiseth me,
   Still all my song shall be,
   Nearer, my God, to thee,
    Nearer to thee.

2 Though like a wanderer,
    Daylight all gone,
   Darkness be over me,
    My rest a stone;
   Yet in my dreams I'd be
   Nearer, my God, to thee.
    Nearer to thee.

3 There let the way appear
    Steps up to heaven:
   All that thou sendest me
    In mercy given;
   Angels to beckon me
   Nearer, my God, to thee,
    Nearer to thee.

21   —o—   KEY G.

1 Precious promise God hath given
   To the weary passer by,
   On the way from earth to heaven
    "I will guide thee with mine eye."

2 When temptations almost win thee,
   And thy trusted watchers fly,
   Let this promise ring within thee,
    "I will guide thee with mine eye."

3 When thy secret hopes have perished
   In the grave of years gone by,
   Let this promise still be cherished,
    "I will guide thee with mine eye."

4 When the shades of night are falling,
   And the hour has come to die,
   Hear thy trusty Pilot calling,
    "I will guide thee with mine eye!"

22   KEY F.

1 In the silent midnight watches,
   List—thy bosom's door!
   How it knocketh, knocketh, knocketh,
    Knocketh evermore!
   Say not 'tis thy pulses beating,
    'Tis thy heart of sin;
   'Tis thy Saviour knocks, and crieth,
    "Rise, and let me in!"

2 Death comes down with reckless foot-
   To the hall and hut;   [steps,
   Think you death will tarry knocking
    When the door is shut?
   Jesus waiteth, waiteth, waiteth;
    But the door is fast;
   Grieved, away thy Saviour goeth,
    Death breaks in at last.

3 Then 'tis time to stand entreating
    Christ to let thee in,
   At the gate of heaven beating,
    Wailing for thy sin!
   Nay! alas, thou guilty creature!
    Hast thou, then, forgot?
   Jesus waited long to know thee,
    Now he knows thee not.

23   HAPPY DAY.—G.

1 O happy day, that fixed my choice
   On thee, my Saviour and my God;
   Well may this glowing heart rejoice,
   And tell its raptures all abroad.

   Happy day, happy day,
  When Jesus washed my sins away!
  He taught me how to watch and pray,
  And live rejoicing every day;
   Happy day, happy day,
  When Jesus washed my sins away!

2 'Tis done, the great transaction's done,
   I am the Lord's, and he is mine;
   He drew me, and I followed on,
   Charmed to confess the voice divine.

3 High heaven, that heard the solemn vow,
   That vow renewed shall daily hear,
   Till in life's latest hour I bow,
   And bless in death a bond so dear.

24   —o—

Jesus, my all to heaven has gone,
He whom I fixed my hopes upon;
His track I see, and I'll pursue
The narrow way, till him I view.
   Happy day, happy day, etc.
    —o—
Then will I tell to sinners round,
What a dear Saviour I have found;
I'll point to thy redeeming blood,
And say, "Behold the way to God."
   Happy day, happy day, etc.

25   KENTUCKY.—A.

1. A charge to keep I have,
A God to glorify,
A never-dying soul to save,
And fit it for the sky.

2. To serve the present age,
My calling to fulfill,—
Oh, may it all my powers engage,
To do my Master's will.

3. Arm me with jealous care,
As in thy sight to live ;
And oh, thy servant, Lord, prepare,
A strict account to give.

4. Help me to watch and pray,
And on thyself rely,
Assured, if I my trust betray
I shall forever die.

26   KEY D.

1. Come, ye disconsolate! where'er ye languish,
Come to the mercy-seat, fervently kneel :
Here bring your wounded hearts, here tell your anguish :
Earth has no sorrow that heaven cannot heal.

2. Joy of the desolate, light of the straying,
Hope of the penitent, fadeless and pure !
Here speaks the Comforter, in God's name saying,—
Earth has no sorrow that heaven cannot cure.

3. Here see the bread of life ; see waters flowing
Forth from the throne of God, boundless in love :
Come to the feast prepared ; come, ever knowing,
Earth has no sorrows but heaven can remove.

27   ROCKINGHAM.—G.

1. Jesus, and shall it ever be,
A mortal man ashamed of thee !
Ashamed of thee, whom angels praise,
Whose glories shine thro' endless days ?

2. Ashamed of Jesus, that dear Friend
On whom my hopes of heaven depend ?
No, when I blush, be this my shame,
That I no more revere his name.

3. Ashamed of Jesus! yes, I may,
When I've no guilt to wash away,
No tear to wipe, no good to crave,
No fear to quell, no soul to save.

4. Till then,—nor is my boasting vain,—
Till then I boast a Saviour slain !
And, oh, may this my glory be,
That Christ is not ashamed of me.

28   WINDHAM.—F.

1. Show pity, Lord, O Lord, forgive ;
Let a repenting rebel live,
Are not thy mercies large and free ?
May not a sinner trust in thee ?

2. My crimes are great, but don't surpass
The power and glory of thy grace ;
Great God, thy nature hath no bound,—
So let thy pard'ning love be found.

3. O wash my soul from every sin,
And make my guilty conscience clean;
Here on my heart the burden lies,
And past offences pain my eyes.

4. My lips with shame my sins confess,
Against thy law, against thy grace ;
Lord, should thy judgments grow severe,
I am condemned, but thou art clear.

29   HEBER.—G.

1. Come, humble sinner, in whose breast
A thousand thoughts revolve,
Come, with your guilt and fear op-
And make this last resolve ; [press'd,

2. I'll go to Jesus, though my sin
Like mountains round me close
I know his courts, I'll enter in,
Whatever may oppose.

3. Prostrate I'll lie before his throne,
And there my guilt confess ;
I'll tell him I'm a wretch undone
Without his sov'reign grace.

4. Perhaps he will admit my plea,
Perhaps will hear my prayer ;
But, if I perish, I will pray,
And perish only there.

5. I can but perish if I go,—
I am resolved to try ;
For if I stay away, I know
I must forever die.

30   AVON—A 2.

1. O for a heart to praise my God,
A heart from sin set free :
A heart that always feels thy blood,
So freely shed for me ;

2. A heart resigned, submissive, meek,
My great Redeemer's throne ;
Where only Christ is heard to speak,
Where Jesus reigns alone.

3. O for a lowly, contrite heart,
Believing, true, and clean ;
Which neither life nor death can part
From him that dwells within ;

A heart in every thought renewed,
And full of love divine ;
Perfect, and right, and pure, and good,
A copy, Lord, of thine.

31 REVIVE US AGAIN.—G.
1 We praise thee, O God, for the Son of
    thy love,
For Jesus, who died, and is now gone above.
Hallelujah! thine the glory, hallelujah!
    Amen. [*again.*
Hallelujah! thine the glory, revive us
2 We praise thee, O God, for thy Spirit of
    light, [tered our night.
Who has shown us our Saviour, and scat-
3 All glory and praise to the Lamb that
    was slain, [every stain.
Who has borne all our sins, and has cleansed

32 ANCHORED FAST—A ♭.
1 Tossing on the billow,
    Rocking in the blast,
  Sick'ning on the pillow,
    Verging t'ward the last.
While the tempest rages,
To the Rock of Ages
I am anchord fast.

2 Skies all clad in sable,
    Storm-clouds scudding past,
  Clinging to the cable,
    Still I'm anchored fast.

3 Gone each earthly treasure,
    Cut away each mast,
  Vanished earthly pleasure,
    Still I'm anchored fast.
                            WM. P. BREED, D.D.

33 REVIVE US AGAIN.—G.
1 Bless the Lord, O my soul, for his mercy
    is great, [estate,
He reached down to save thee from thy lost
Praise and bless him, bless and praise him,
    His name magnify! [*high.*
O my soul, bless thy Saviour, who liveth on
2 Bless the Lord, O my soul, by his wis-
    dom and power
He guides thee, and guards thee, and keeps
    thee each hour.
3 Bless the Lord, O my soul, he hath sealed
    thee his own,
And will send down his angels to bring thee
    safe home.
4 Bless the Lord, O my soul, it thy priv'-
    ledge shall be
To praise him and laud him thro' eternity.
                                       H. F. M.

34 OH, 'TIS GLORY.—E ♭.
1 To thy cross, dear Christ, I'm clinging,
    All my refuge and my plea;
  Matchless is thy loving-kindness,
    Else it had not stoop'd to me.
Oh, 'tis glory! oh, 'tis glory!
Oh, 'tis glory in my soul!
For I've touched the hem of his garment,
And his pow'r doth make me whole.

2 Long my heart hath heard thee calling,
    But I thrust aside thy grace;
  Yet, oh, boundless condescension!
    Love is shining from thy face.

3 Love eternal, light eternal,
    Close me safely, sweetly in;
  Saviour, let thy balm of healing
    Ever keep me free from sin.
            FLORA L. BEST. From *Gems of Praise.*

35 TITLE CLEAR.—G.
1 While sailing o'er life's stormy sea,
  The hope of heaven how sweet to me,
  It fills my soul with extacy,
    This blood-bought hope of heaven.
  When clouds are lowering dark and drear,
  And sorrows surging waves appear,
  To feel my blessed Saviour near
    Gives me this hope of heaven.
We'll stand the storm, it won't be very long,
    We'll anchor by and by.

2 Blow then, ye storms, ye thunders roll,
  My Jesus shall your power control,
  And he has planted in my soul
    This cheering hope of heaven.
  With him on board I fear no harm,
  Secure from danger and alarm,
  I have, while leaning on his arm,
    A glorious hope of heaven.
                                JAS. NICHOLSON

36 NEW OVER THERE.—B ♭.
1 They have reached the sunny shore,
  And will never hunger more;
    All their grief and pains are o'er,
      Over there;
  And they need no lamp by night,
  For their day is always bright,
  And their Saviour is their light,
      Over there.
Over there, over there,
They can never know a fear over there;
All their streets are shining gold,
And their glory is untold;
'Tis the Savior's blissful fold, over there

2 Now they feel no-chilling blast.
  For their winter-time is past,
  And their summers always last,
      Over there;
  They can never know a fear,
  For the Savior's always near,
  And with them is endless cheer,
      Over there.

3 They have fought the weary fight,
  Jesus saved them by his might,
  Now they dwell with him in light,
      Over there;
  Soon we'll reach the shining strand,
  But we'll wait our Lord's command,
  Till we see his beck'ning hand,
      Over there.

INDEX.

Titles in Capitals: First Lines in Roman.

A

	PAGE.
A charge to keep I have	116
A cry comes over the deep	46
A joy unknown to my poor soul	33
Alas! and did my Saviour bleed?	56
All hail the power of Jesus' name	113
ALL TO CHRIST I OWE	55
Am I a soldier of the cross?	96
ANCHORED FAST	117
ARE YOU READY?	26
ASBURY PARK	35
A vision bright appeared to me	16
Awake, my soul, in joyful lays	114

B

BEAUTIFUL LAND	84
Behold him standing at the door	71
BELIEVING	56
BEULAH LAND	69
Bless the Lord, O my soul	117
Blest be the tie that binds	110
Brightest and best of the sons of the...	98
Brothers! rally for the conflict	105

C

Children of the heavenly King	77
Christians, I am on my journey	29
CHRIST THE LORD IS RISEN	92
CHRIST OUR LEADER	77
CLINGING AND RESTING	32
COME AND SIGN	103
Come and sign the pledge to-night	107
Come, every soul by sin oppressed	42
Come, for the invitation	51
Come, humble sinner, in whose breast	116
COME QUICK AND TAKE ME O'ER	14
Come, thou fount of every blessing	108
COME TO THE ROYAL FOUNTAIN	94
Come, ye disconsolate! where'er ye	116

D

	PAGE.
DAUGHTER OF ZION	20
Dear Jesus, I long to be perfectly	54
DEATH IS THERE	104
DELIVERANCE WILL COME	50
Do we always tell the Story?	82

E

ENDLESS PRAISE	17
EVEN ME	53

F

FAITHFUL GUIDE	81
Father, whate'er of earthly bliss	112
Fierce was the billow wild	30
FREEDOM'S FLAG	18
From the Riven Rock there floweth	45
From every stormy wind that blows	109

G

GATHER LIFE'S ROSES	24
Glorious things of thee are spoken	29
Go bury thy sorrow	31
GOING HOME	97
GRATEFUL PRAISE	89
Guide me, O thou great Jehovah	113

H

Hark, the glad sound, the Saviour	111
Hark, 'tis the watchman's cry	72
HEAVENLY VISION	16
He came to the banks of the Jordan	38
He leadeth me, oh, blessed thought!	97
HE WILL GATHER THE WHEAT, &C.	25
Holy Spirit, faithful guide	81
HOME IN THE SWEET BY AND BY	62
Ho, my comrades, see the signal	58
HOME OF THE SOUL	71
How lovely is Jesus, the Lamb that	43

(118)

INDEX.

I

I am a little soldier	85
I am waiting, O my Father	42
I bring my sins to thee	75
I find no weary hours	63
I gave my life for thee	45
I have a Saviour, he's pleading in	113
I have longed for the bliss of pardon	57
I hear the Saviour say	55
I hear thy welcome voice	114
I know not what shall befall me	66
I'LL ENTER THE OPEN DOOR	57
I love to sing of Jesus	83
I Love to Tell the Story	52
I love to trust in Jesus	61
I'M A PILGRIM GOING HOME	29
In faithful bonds united	19
In gospel armor now I stand	88
In the Rifted Rock I'm resting	95
In the silent midnight watches	115
I saw a wayworn traveller	50
I SHALL BE SATISFIED	65
IS MY NAME WRITTEN THERE?	70
IT REACHES ME	96
I'VE BEEN REDEEMED	55
I've reached the land of corn and	69
I will sing you a song of a beautiful	71

J

Jerusalem, thy mansions fair	44
Jesus, and shall it ever be	116
Jesus, I my cross have taken	28
JESUS, LOVE ME STILL	48
Jesus, lover of my soul	35
Jesus, my all, to heaven has gone	115
Jesus, my Lord, to thee I cry	60
Jesus, thine all-victorious love	56
Joy to the world, the Lord is come	111
JOY UNKNOWN	33
Just as I am, without one plea	60

K

Knocking, knocking, who is there?	114

L

LEANING ON JESUS	27
Let us gather up the sunbeams	59
Let us praise the Lord	89
LET US SEEK SALVATION TO-DAY	91
LIGHT AFTER DARKNESS	37
LITTLE SOLDIER	85
Lord, dismiss us with thy blessing	110
Lord, I care not for riches	70
Lord, I hear of showers of blessing	53
Lord, we come before thee now	35
Lo! the day of rest declineth	108
LOVING JESUS	83

M

MIGHTY TO SAVE	68
MORE LIKE THEE	76
MORNING, NOON, AND NIGHT	34
Must Jesus bear the cross alone	109
MY ALL TO THEE	75
My days are gliding swiftly by	39
My faith looks up to thee	113
My feet are in the water	14
My hope is built on nothing less	114
My soul, be on thy guard	80

N

Nearer, my God, to thee	115
NO LOVE LIKE THE LOVE OF JESUS	28
No night in heaven	17
NOT KNOWING	66

O

O for a heart to praise my God	116
O for a thousand tongues, to sing	111
Oh, do not let the Word depart	47
Oh, happy day, that fixed my choice	114
Oh, mariners, what dangers	86
Oh, sometimes the shadows are deep	114
Oh, think of the home over there	113
Oh, this uttermost salvation	96
OH, 'TIS GLORY IN MY SOUL	117
Oh, touch it not! for deep within	104
Oh, what utter darkness	48
Oh, who is this that cometh	68
Oh, wonderful river!	64
On Jordan's stormy banks I stand	67
ONLY TRUST HIM	42
ON THE SHOALS	46
Our Country's flag! O, emblem dear	18
OVER THERE	113

P

PEACE, IT IS I	30
Prayer is the key	72
PRECIOUS PROMISE	115

R

REMEMBER JESUS LEADS	78
RESCUE THE PERISHING	31
REVIVE US AGAIN	117
Rock of Ages, cleft for me	114

S

Saviour, make me more like thee	76
Say, brother, will you meet us	107
SCATTER SEEDS OF KINDNESS	59
See, in the vineyard of the Lord	41
See, the purple wine is flowing	100

INDEX.

See where the living waters glide	94
Shall we gather at the river?	58
SHALL WE MEET BEYOND THE RIVER,	36
Should the summons, quickly flying	26
Show pity, Lord, O Lord, forgive	116
SIGN THE PLEDGE	107
SO MUCH LIKE JESUS,	39
SOUND THE BATTLE CRY	102
Sowing the seed by the daylight fair	113
Stand up and bless the Lord	81
Stand up, stand up for Jesus	79
STAR OF THE EAST,	98
STORM THE FORT,	58
Sweet hour of prayer	112

T

TAKE ME AS I AM	60
TENDER SHEPHERD	49
THE ALTOGETHER LOVELY	43
THE BARREN FIG-TREE	41
THE DRUNKARD'S CHILD	106
The Great Physician now is here	80
THE GOLDEN KEY	72
THE INVITATION,	51
THE LAND JUST ACCROSS THE RIVER	67
THE LODE STAR	86
THE NEW JERUSALEM	44
THE NEW NAME	87
THE NEW SONG	74
THE PERFECT WAY	63
There are songs of joy that I loved to.	74
There is a fountain filled with blood	112
There is a gate that stands ajar	112
There is no love like the love of Jesus.	28
There's a home in the sweet by and by	62
There's a land of peerless brightness	97
THE RIFTED ROCK	95
THE RIVER OF JORDAN	38
THE RIVER OF LIFE	64
THE SAVIOUR AT THE DOOR	71
THE SMITTEN ROCK	45

THE SYREN'S SONG	100
THE VALIANT SOLDIER	88
THE WATCHMAN'S CRY	72
do. do. Male Voices.	73
They have reached the sunny shore	117
To-day the Saviour calls	113
To Father, Son and Holy Ghost	111
Tossing on the billow	117
To the cross I long was clinging	32
To thy cross, dear Christ, I'm clinging	117

W

WASHED IN THE BLOOD OF THE LAMB	36
Weary with walking alone	27
Welcome, welcome, dear Redeemer	108
We love to hear the story	90
We never shall be happy if we walk	91
We praise thee, O God	117
We shall have a new name	87
WE SHALL KNOW	40
What a Friend we have in Jesus	112
What hast thou done for me?	45
What is it that adorns the daily life	39
What Shall the Harvest be?	112
When I shall wake in that fair morn	65
When Jesus shall gather the nations	25
When the mists have rolled,	40
When the rosy tints of morning	34
While sailing o'er life's stormy sea	117
White as snow, oh, what a promise	36
WHITER THAN SNOW	54
Who hath sorrow, who hath woe?	105
WHY NOT TO-NIGHT?	47
Work, for the night is coming	115
Wrecked! 'tis a feeble word	101

Y

Ye soldiers, to the charge go forth	78
Yield not to Temptation	79
You ask me why so oft, papa	106

www.ingramcontent.com/pod-product-compliance
Lightning Source LLC
Chambersburg PA
CBHW020129170426
43199CB00010B/698